# Happiness

# Happiness
## Always and in All Ways

**Just *Win* Singh**

# Viva Books

New Delhi | Mumbai | Chennai | Kolkata | Bengaluru | Hyderabad | Kochi | Guwahati

## Publisher's note

First Published 2012

## Viva Books Private Limited

- 4737/23, Ansari Road, Daryaganj, New Delhi 110 002
  Tel. 42242200, 23258325, 23283121, Email: vivadelhi@vivagroupindia.net

- 76, Service Industries, Shirvane, Sector 1, Nerul, Navi Mumbai 400 706
  Tel. 27721273, 27721274, Email: vivamumbai@vivagroupindia.net

- Jamals Fazal Chambers, 26 Greams Road, Chennai 600 006
  Tel. 28294241, 28290304, Email: vivachennai@vivagroupindia.net

- B-103, Jindal Towers, 21/1A/3 Darga Road, Kolkata 700 017
  Tel. 22816713, Email: vivakolkata@vivagroupindia.net

- 7, GF, Sovereign Park Aptts., 56-58, K. R. Road, Basavanagudi, Bengaluru 560 004
  Tel. 26607409, Email: vivabangalore@vivagroupindia.net

- 101-102, Moghal Marc Apartments, 3-4-637 to 641, Narayanguda, Hyderabad 500 029
  Tel. 27564481, Email: vivahyderabad@vivagroupindia.net

- First Floor, Beevi Towers, SRM Road, Kaloor, Kochi 682 018
  Tel. 0484-2403055, 2403056, Email: vivakochi@vivagroupindia.net

- 232, GNB Road, Beside UCO Bank, Silpukhuri, Guwahati 781 003
  Tel. 0361-2666386, Email: vivaguwahati@vivagroupindia.net

*www.vivagroupindia.com*

ISBN: 978-81-309-2036-8

Published by Vinod Vasishtha for Viva Books Private Limited, 4737/23 Ansari Road, Daryaganj, New Delhi 110 002.

Printed & bound by Raj Press, R-3, Inderpuri, New Delhi 110 012.

This book is dedicated to all the lovely people who take the
RESPONSIBILITY of living a HAPPIER LIFE…



Who choose to BE A BLESSING
Rather than trying to get blessed…



Who know that they do not need to HAVE a good day
For they can always MAKE A GOOD DAY!!



May this book empower you further in your commitment to
Live a Bigger, Better and a more Meaningful Life!!

# CONTENTS

# PREFACE

When I started the INSTITUTE OF HAPPINESS in Vadodara, India, it happened as if Life wanted it so.

A friend of mine who had taken all possible help from personal and professional sources was on the verge of contemplating suicide. Life had gotten him down and discouraged in all areas of his life – professional, personal, financial and physical. (he actually went through a heart attack at the tender age of 33 years.)

When I met him and discussed with him at length, he was somehow able to see life in a new perspective. Within days of doing what I suggested, he could see improvement in himself and all walks of his life.

After exactly 32 days of my initial meeting with him, he actually flew down to Vadodara just to kiss my hand and tell me that his LIFE WAS GREAT!! He confirmed that the simple suggestions I gave him *changed his life* when all others had failed him.

Though I was humbled by the way he gave me all the credit for the work he had actually done (for I knew that all I had really done was just give him simple suggestions), I felt that Life was giving me feedback that probably this is why I came on this beautiful planet. Probably I had been gifted to tell the truths of life in a simple, usable way.

Inspired by my friend's prompting to not take this gift lightly, I founded the INSTITUTE OF HAPPINESS in 2000. From then on there was no looking back. (For more details on our activities please log onto www.instituteofhappiness.com.)

Over the years, our Institute was able to assist hundreds of people across the globe to a happier life. In fact, our BE HAPPY Course booklets became an instant hit in India and abroad.

People demanded that it was time I wrote a book and so in 2009 I came out with our first book *Happiness Gain & Retain*.

Many people, known and strangers, have written to us, called us and thanked us for taking out the book. Soon, there was impatient pressure from our readers requesting us for more.

Hence this book!!

I personally feel that this book was channeled through my being but written by a power greater than I can ever imagine.

Go ahead then and enjoy another DOSE OF GOODNESS!! May you be happy always and in all ways!!

Just *Win* Singh

# 1

# We Are a Uni-Verse

## Inspiring thoughts

- Regardless of where any of us is on this globe, given a world that is round, it is impossible to choose up sides.

  *—Dr Wayne Dyer*

- We are not simply machines trying to reach a destination. We are hearts and souls vibrantly connected to everyone and everything around us each moment of every day.

  *—Author Unknown*

- Never doubt that a small group of thoughtful, committed citizens can change the world. Indeed, it is the only thing that ever has.

  *—Margaret Mead*

- If not now, when? If not you, who?

  *—Jewish saying*

- The sole meaning of life is to serve humanity.

  *—Leo Tolstoy*

- To discover joy is to return to a state of oneness with the Universe.

  *—Peggy Jenkins*

- People say 'I want peace.' If you remove the I (ego) and your want (desire), you are left with peace.

  *—Satya Sai Baba*

- Once you make a decision, the Universe conspires to make it happen.

  *—Emerson*

- You know you have won, when you love everyone.

  *—Just Win Singh*

Just think for a minute – What is the major reason we are unhappy today? It is because we are feeling separate from all creation. We have lost touch with our Unity of Existence.

And the truth is that Happiness is in Unity!

The saints of ancient India who lived *naturally* happy and healthy lives, practiced YOGA which literally mean 'UNITY.'

So, to begin with we will need to remove certain limitations set in our minds, to free us to a happier perspective of life. We begin this journey with the unique 'principle of oneness.'

You love your country? Great! But why not love the whole world, of which your country is just a part? You love your religion and your community people? Wonderful! But how about appreciating every other religion and all other communities with equal love which is the core message being preached to you by your religion ie. to LOVE ALL?

You love your family? Excellent! But what if you developed a feeling that every human being on this planet is a member of your family? Wouldn't you no more feel 'alone' even when you were away from home?

Understand the fact that just like you love your country, so does everybody else love theirs; just like you honour your religion, so do all others honour theirs; just like you are intensely attached to your family, so is everybody else connected with his family.

Then why go about trying to prove that your country, your religion, your community, your family, etc. is better than the rest? Why not take pride of being a member of the World Family? Why not simply focus on being a good child of Mother Earth? Why try to cut off each other rather than live to enhance each individual's experience of life?

We have to and must understand that we are all separate fingers of the same hand of humanity and we are hurting today (all of us) because we do not want to remain a part of the hand *but each finger wants to become the hand itself.*

All human violence is a direct reflection of our belief in our separation. And till we realize that we are all one and that God is within each of us, we will continue to harm each other, and in the process, stay unhappy ourselves.

While reading this chapter, look at the mega picture of the World and you will be able to hit on the single greatest cause of unhappiness. Once you put the principle of oneness into practice, you will start feeling more 'human' than you ever felt before.

*Stop being proud to just own your house when you can easily own the whole world.* May God give you the humbleness needed to understand this necessary concept of happiness!!

> *You are a fish which is thirsty in the ocean.*
> —Kabir

## STORY-TIME

*Two friends were out on the lake in a row boat. One took a small hand drill from his pocket, and began to drill a hole in the floor of the boat.*

*His friend was flabbergasted. 'Are you crazy? What are you doing? You will make a hole in the bottom of the boat, the water will flood in, the boat will sink, and we will drown.'*

*The man with the drill replied, 'Don't worry. I am just drilling the hole under my seat.'*

The above story awakens us directly to the truth that we have become so self-centered that we have forgotten that we were put on this planet together for a reason. If even one of us behaves selfishly, we could end up destroying everybody else.

Each of us is behaving like a cancer cell. A cancer cell is an organism that has no reference to the whole body. It lives separately and does not cooperate with the other cells of the body. What happens ultimately? The whole body dies along with the cancer cell. Who gains? Nobody!

## WHY ARE WE BEHAVING LIKE CANCER CELLS?

Have you ever heard a tree say, 'Here is oxygen only for the people I like?' A mango tree never says, 'I won't give you mangoes because you don't like me.' The trees simply invite everybody to help themselves to whatever they have to offer.

It is only we human beings who are so biased and selfish in sharing what we have. We always want to choose who deserves and who doesn't and this leads to our separatist psychology. Unfortunately, each one of us has been taught by our so-called cultured society that separateness is the essence of humanity. We have been conditioned to believe in boundaries, customs and traditions. *We are no more simply humans.*

Instead, we proudly identify ourselves as Indian, French, German, male, female, upper class, etc. These are all labels that classify us as separate from the 'others'. So the 'others' almost become like our competitors who must be 'beaten' in some way or the other (pun intended) so that we can prove ourselves to be superior to 'them.' This feeling of separation from each other allows humans to do all manner of things to each other that they would (ironically) never do to themselves.

We are trying to co-create life APART instead of co-creating it TOGETHER. This is why we have conflict, discord, war and hatred. This is the reason why we spite, compete and argue with each other. This is why we are living in an unhappy world.

*None of us sees life as it is. We all see life as WE are.* We look at others through our own likes and dislikes, prejudices, desires and interest. It is this separatist outlook that fragments life for us – man against woman, community against community, country against country, religion against religion.

Such an attitude has made our mind-set focused on division rather than unity, which has been proven throughout our history that has records of us always being at war with one another. *If humanity is always choosing to be at war, how can human beings ever be happy then?*

## HOW ONENESS MAKES YOU HAPPY?

Try this exercise:

When you see someone who appears separate from you, look at him deeply. Look *into* him. When you do this for a few seconds consciously, you will meet 'you' waiting there, in him. That will prove your connection with that person. But you must do this exercise sincerely and with an open mind.

If you can feel the oneness with this person, start practicing in the same way with other people who seem different to you. A time will come when you can see yourself in every person you meet. (You will see they all have your kind of desires, your kind of behaviours, and a similar thirst of finding the clue to being happy.)

When you will see nothing but 'you' wherever you look, you will then peer through the eyes of the Creator. As your sense of oneness increases, pain and disappointment will miraculously disappear from your life. Why? Because suffering is a response to separation and sorrow is an announcement of its truth.

## WHAT NEEDS TO BE DONE?

The chaos of society (which is ensuring that our planet evolves into a collection of disconnected components) needs to be cleared with effort from each individual.

We must understand and teach our children that we are a Universe.

The word was formed from *'Uni'* meaning 'one' and *'Verse'* meaning 'song.' So literally we are 'one song.' And if we do not want cacophony, we must sing this song harmoniously. Our planet is like a beautiful garden. We are all individual flowers in it. Our different colours, shapes and sizes simply add to the beauty of this planet. We can and should, therefore, value the various differences among ourselves – such as differences in our physical features, talents, cultures, religions, etc. We must never allow these differences to blind us to our fundamental oneness as human beings.

Since our civilized culture has failed us over and over again, it's now time to change things. You and I, who make the body of humanity complete, must work in harmony with each other as a common body. We, as awakened souls, need to spread the importance of love and kindness, faith and hope, compassion and non violence to people who are still blinded with their selfishness.

We need to awaken everyone to remember that we are all 'one song' and so must treat each other with respect and dignity, not as bodies to be climbed over on the road of material success.

*Start living in complete harmony with every other living being on this earth.* Suddenly you will feel the connectedness you had missed for so many years because someone conditioned your mind to go into the world to prove yourself as a superior human being. There is no need for you to prove that.

By merely spreading the message of oneness, you will be more receptive to every single human being and that is when you will start living in the blissful state of eternal happiness for *you will no more have any enemies left in this world.* And if the whole world is your friend, how can you be sad?

Begin by implementing this concept in your own life from today. Feel the difference of 'owning' this world (rather than just your house) and you will then know what it means to work for God. As all our scriptures emphasize, 'The highest feeling is the experience of unity with all that is.'

Remember, we are all children of God who has no favourites. Look through the eyes of the God within you and you will see – we are ALL ONE.

## I COULD HAVE CHANGED THE WORLD

*When I was a young man,*
*I wanted to change the world.*
*I found it was difficult to change the world,*
*So I tried to change my nation.*
*When I found I couldn't change the nation,*
*I began to focus on my town.*
*I couldn't change the town and as an older man,*
*I tried to change my family.*
*Now, as an old man, I realize*
*One thing I can change is myself.*
*And suddenly I realize that if long ago*
*I had changed myself,*
*I could have made an impact on my family.*
*My family and I could have made*
*An impact on our town.*

*Their impact could have changed the nation*
*And I could indeed have…*
*Changed the world!*

—*Author Unknown*

Something soulful

## A HUMAN BEING

A human being is a part of the whole,
Called by us 'Universe';
A part limited in time and space.
He experiences himself, his thoughts and feelings
As something separate from the rest –
A kind of optical delusion of consciousness.

This delusion is a kind of prison for us,
Restricting us to our personal desires
And to affection for a few persons nearest to us.

Our task must be to free ourselves from this prison
By widening our circle of compassion
To embrace all living creatures and
The whole of Nature in its beauty.

—*Albert Einstein*

## BUILD A BETTER YOU

'You should build a better world,' God said.
He questioned 'How?
The World is such a wondrous place
So complicated now!
And I so small and useless am,
There's nothing I can do.'
But God, all-wise and kind replied:
'Just build a better you.'

*—Alexander Pope*

## MAKE THE WHOLE WORLD BETTER

To make the whole world better,
Here's all you have to do –
Start to be a brother
To the man that's next to you.

*—Author Unknown*

## Action plan

1) From now onwards, simply view yourself as a human being. Practice basic spirituality by thinking globally and acting locally.

> Consciously start emphasizing on the fact that it's all right to remain without any labels of religion, country, etc. *but its more important to be a good and sensible human being, with basic human qualities of goodness, kindness, compassion, caring,* and live with a sense of responsibility for making this a better and happier world.

2) Consider every single person in the world as your friend. Feel the great joy of embracing humanity in totality.

> *Practice meeting everybody as a member of your family (of humanity).* When you know no strangers, then even your worst enemy cannot make you feel that you are not a friend. When that awakening comes, you will feel the great state of happiness and joy in loving all that is.

*'You have a right to be proud of your town,' a visitor observed to the hotel clerk. 'I was especially impressed with the number of temples. Surely the people here must love the Lord.'*
*'Well,' replied the hotel clerk hesitantly, 'they may love the Lord, but they sure as hell hate each other!'*

# 2
# Drop the Ego

## Inspiring thoughts

- No one can make you feel inferior without your permission.
  —*Eleanor Roosevelt*

- Egotism is the anesthetic that deadens the pain of stupidity.
  —*Knute Rockne*

- I learned a long time ago never to wrestle with a pig. You get dirty and besides, the pig likes it.
  —*Cyrus Ching*

- If you are all wrapped up in yourself, you are over dressed.
  —*Kate Halverson*

- Ego: the fallacy where the goose thinks he's a swan.
  —*Author Unknown*

- The nice thing about egotists is that they don't talk about other people.
  —*Lucille Harper*

- Big egos are big shields for lots of empty space.
  —*Diana R Black*

- It is the nature of ego to take, and the nature of spirit to share.
  —*Proverb*

- Talent is God given – be humble. Fame is man given – be grateful. Conceit is self given – be careful.
  —*John Wooden*

- We are unhappy because we look for external solutions to internal problems.
  —*Just* Win *Singh*

If you have started applying the principle of oneness which we talked about in our previous chapter, you must have found it to be one of the most difficult tasks you have ever undertaken.

You would have observed that nearly everybody is so EGOISTIC that there seems little chance to improve things. It is because the true culprit of unhappiness is the EGO.

Nothing causes more pain and suffering than your ego. *Increase your ego and you increase your suffering.* Very few factors can contribute more to your stress, anxiety and frustration than a large ego. Therefore, easing off your ego is one of the most leveraged efforts you can make to enjoy life.

Ego is very harmful to internal harmony. It is like a dictator whose goal is not the good of the country, but the preservation of its own power. And hunger for power can never open the doors to happiness. It can only lead one into a sadistic, unsatisfied thirst for more.

Many people are confused regards the difference between the ego and pride. Well, simply put, *the ego gives you a swollen head while pride gives you a swollen heart.* A big head gives you a big headache whereas a big heart makes you humble.

With this chapter we encourage you to drop off your ego if you wish to experience bliss in your life. Dropping off your ego is accomplished by your INTENTION. You must have the desire to shrink your ego down and to see how destructive it is to your happiness. All it takes is humility and patience.

Once you are free of ego, you will be able to see your fellow humans as they are rather than as you think they should be. The more you desire joy and happiness, the less your ego will have to be and the day your ego is no more, the whole of heaven will be in your grasp.

Your ego encourages you to remain self-centred and it feels pinched when you try to serve others with no thought of any gain.

That's why the people who really want to help others, have no ego and are totally humble people.

If each of us can become more humble, sincere and generous, wouldn't the world be a much nicer and happier place to live in? Think about it!

Stop Edging God Out, and start appreciating your true inner self. Only then can you truly live the happy life God intended you to live.

> *Do not put all your ego in one basket.*
> —R V Harms

## STORY-TIME

*Once a monk was talking about humility. A villager listening to him got up and said, 'You are nothing. I know a man who is more humble than you.'*

*Suddenly, anger caused by ego, rose inside the monk and he said, 'Who is that man? Show him to me.'*

*'That is not the point,' the villager told him; 'that is not the point. I am not going to show him to you. But try to understand, because suddenly the ego comes in and says, "How can somebody else dare to be more humble than me?"'*

Whenever any person is easily offended, it is his self-absorbed ego that gets hurt and insists on proving how special and important he is. *When ego is offended, it needs revenge.* It needs to retaliate to demonstrate its importance and specialness. And whenever anybody lives in this mode of proving himself as a better human being, he tends to disconnect from the love of his fellow beings and that's when unhappiness creeps in to throw his inner harmony out of his body of peace.

# WHAT IS THE EGO?

Ego is that part of us that needs to stand out and be special. Though each one of us is certainly special in our own unique way, our ego has *the need* to prove this to everyone. How is the ego born? The ego is an accumulated phenomenon, a by-product of living with others. Our parents or society encouraged us since childhood to
- always prove ourselves to be right
- strive to ensure we have more things
- defeat others to be winners in life
- count our awards and badges of honour as our level of success
- trust no one
- fight others, as life is a game of survival of the fittest
- suspect others if they intend to do some good for us…

This list of antiquated beliefs is endless and has the greatest effect on our life. This conditioning was passed down to us directly since we were scared little children and did not have the power to decide what was correct. We simply believed every word we were taught.

If since childhood we have been taught to 'beware of others' then our entire beginning has been based on separateness and superiority. That's when we developed our need to prove ourselves and that's when our ego started developing like a devil of haughtiness inside us.

# WHY MUST WE DROP THE EGO?

Sadly for humanity, each one of us develops a strong level of ego by the time we reach adulthood. Our ego becomes so powerful that it makes us feel outraged when we are wronged, insulted when we are not appreciated, offended when we do not succeed in something and hurt when we lose a contest or an argument.

This insanity of the ego encourages us to pursue our vendettas of hatred and once hatred sets in, happiness disappears thus making us feel incompetent, insecure, inadequate, stupid, unworthy and sometimes evil. This destroys our self-esteem and produces doubt of our self-worth in our own eyes. This leads us to become self-centred, self-concerned and hard to get along with.

We then start spending time and energy concerned about how others may be viewing us and do our best to get outward appreciation. We buy all sorts of things (cars, clothes, perfumes…) in order to just gain attention. Our ego even encourages us to argue and fight because it wants to be noticed; it wants attention, *even if by trouble-making.*

The ego makes us self-centred and develops our need to scream 'LOOK AT ME!' Because of our self-centredness we lose our compassion for and interest in others. We stay in the beggar's mode of 'what's-in-it-for-me.' This attitude in life can never supply anybody with the heart-expanding joy of creating a wonderful and happy life.

*Anybody who acts in destructive or aggressive ways towards people is actually a person who lacks inner harmony.* And one of the surest ways to develop inner harmony is by dropping the ego.

There is a lot you will gain by dropping your ego. You will feel as though a huge burden has been lifted from your head. You will stop putting your energy in efforts to be on guard and in trying to prove things. Thus you will have a great deal more energy for positive things in life and will become more light-hearted.

Furthermore, as your ego reduces, you will become more interested in other people. You will tend to become a better listener with more kindness in your nature. This will translate into people liking you even more than they already do. Wouldn't that make you happier?

## HOW TO DROP THE EGO?

*If fear is your constant companion, then you quite surely are in the clutches of the ego.* When the focus of your life is fear-based you tend to believe that your value is based on your performance. If you perform well, you are worthy; if you fail to perform well, you are worthless. This fear drives you to perform better and better in order to validate yourself. This fear makes you feel disappointed and offended if you fail to receive when you give, because you do what you do just for gaining a positive feedback about yourself.

Virtually all fears can be traced directly back to self-esteem. If you love yourself, you will be able to transform your fears with love rather than allow them to direct your life. *So, the first and foremost thing in your life is self-acceptance.* You must love yourself for who you are and you must be yourself anywhere at any time. Only when you love yourself can you fully participate in life.

When you have adequate self-esteem, slighting remarks will have little effect on you – you will simply pass over and ignore them. Remember, you will always be a failure in someone's eyes. You simply cannot please everyone, so learn to please yourself and start relishing the person you are.

The most valuable thing you can ever own is your image of yourself as a winner in the great game of life, as a contributor to the betterment of mankind, and as an achiever of worthy goals. Unless you have that image of yourself, nothing worth having will stay with you for long.

Stop living as you think you are supposed to in order to be accepted by others. Instead, start finding out who you really are. Awaken to your true self. There is nothing to fear when you know that you are already divine and complete and do not have to do anything to prove it.

Remember, you don't have to try to be any specific something somebody else would want. *Just plain goodness is your basic quality for being attractive to all people.*

Definitely compete in a competition but never feel the need to empower those you compete with. Enjoy all your possessions but don't become possessed by them.

Heaven on Earth begins happening when you abandon the false idea that you need to prove to anyone that you have acquired the necessary credentials…TO BE CONSIDERED A SUCCESS!!

## HOW SELFISH WE CAN BE

*The mind always thinks in terms of the self.*
*It is egocentric.*
*During the French Revolution*
*A man from Paris stopped at a village*
*And was asked by a friend what was happening.*
*'They are cutting off heads by the thousands,'*
*Said the visitor.*
*'How terrible!' cried the villager,*
*'That could ruin my hat business.'*

—*Author Unknown*

Something soulful

## EGO

When you are feeling high and mighty
And your ego is supreme;
When you feel like the King of Blighty
And everybody's dream.

Just pause, and think this over,
You are not an irreplaceable bloke;
You are not as rare as a three-leaf clover,
You are less useful than a cloak.

Take a bucket, fill it with water from the rains
And dip your hands to the wrist;
Pull it out and the hole that remains
Measures how much you will be missed.

When you entered this world, you cry and you turn,
You stir up a messy score;
But when you go, will you be amazed to learn
That the world's quite the same as before.

The moral, it's quite so clear,
Is to do the best service you can;
Be humble and just wipe off a tear
And don't think you are an indispensable man.

—*Digonadas*

## THE ONLY PRACTICAL SOLUTION

My stand is clear –
Produce to distribute,
Feed before you eat,
Give before you take,
Think of others before you think of yourself.
Only a selfless society based on sharing
Can be stable and happy;
This is the only practical solution.
If you do not want it, then –
Fight.

—*Nisargdatta Maharaj*

## Action plan

1)  One of the best ways to tame the ego is to give more of your self and ask less in return.

> Once you make serving others your priority, *start focusing on 'How may I serve?' rather than on 'How can I get?'* You will then have no expectations about how others respond to your acts of love. You will become too busy in your mission of spreading goodness simply for experiencing love yourself.

2)  Listen to your heart before you react to anybody. Try to tame your ego at least once today.

> Before speaking, ask yourself, 'Is what I am about to say for the purpose of making someone else wrong and proving myself right or special? *Will I end up creating more turmoil or more serenity?'* Then make the decision to be kind and loving…no matter what.

> *A man and his wife were coming out from a cocktail party and the man said, 'Darling, has anybody ever told you how fascinating, how beautiful, how wonderful you are?'*
>
> *His wife felt very, very good and was very happy. She said, 'I wonder why nobody has ever told me this?'*
>
> *The man replied, 'Then where did you get the idea?'*

# 3

## Control Anger

## Inspiring thoughts

- Speak when you are angry and you will make the best speech you will ever regret.

  *—Ambrose Bierce*

- Resentment is like taking poison and waiting for the other person to die.

  *—Malachy McCourt*

- For every minute you remain angry, you give up sixty seconds of peace of mind.

  *—Ralph Waldo Emerson*

- Focus on pulling out the arrow rather than spending time wondering who shot it.

  *—Dalai Lama*

- If a small thing has the power to make you angry, does that not indicate something about your size?

  *—Sydney J. Harris*

- Revenge is often like biting a dog because the dog bit you.

  *—Austin O'Malley*

- Whatever is begun in anger, ends in shame.

  *—Benjamin Franklin*

- A man is about as big as the things that make him angry.

  *—Winston Churchill*

- Why spend energy in *harming* someone? Why not spend energy in *charming* someone?

  *—Just* Win *Singh*

It is time to take up a stance to face another great challenge... that of controlling anger. This task is like trying to control a fire-emitting dragon with an ice-box on your head. But, if your ice-box is effective and your determination is convincing, this dragon will soon give up. All the best!

*Like all emotions, anger is the result of thinking.* If you think you have been wronged or misjudged, you tend to get angry. Anger obscures your mind and makes your everyday life unhappy. While your anger is strong, you can think of nothing other than harm. And once you get this thought of destroying the object of your anger, you spit venom which disrupts any chance for your experiencing peace.

Unfortunately, anger is one of the most poorly handled emotion in our society. Even though anger is one of the most common emotions known to the human race, few of us are skilled at responding to this feeling with complete effectiveness.

We all know that *anger is just a 'D' away from Danger* and still very few of us bother to do something about this emotion. This lesson is aimed at motivating you to get up and take charge. Stop letting your anger control your happiness. Instead, be sure to keep it under control. If you can keep your cool when others are losing theirs, you will always be the 'solutions-man' who will be looked up for being mature enough to have your emotions in control.

Then something miraculous will happen. Not only will people respect you more, many will try to duplicate your behaviour. Once many people start choosing to stay cool, they will send out a wave of peace in their vicinity which could grow so big that a time may probably come when we will choose love over hatred *every time.*

That will be the day when Nature will smile back on us and be happy that finally we have all chosen the path of love...which is the most natural human emotion. That will be the end of hatred.

That will be the end of war. And that will be the end of pessimism. That day will be the beginning of universal happiness.

Only positive people have positive dreams and missions. If you are sneering at the thought of eradication of hatred, you are the one who needs this lesson the most. Assume then, that this lesson has been dedicated to you…and for the sake of your happiness…realize the importance of what is being highlighted. It's your only chance to get on the road of happiness.

> *He who angers you conquers you.*
> —Elizabeth Kenny

## STORY-TIME

*There was a little boy with a bad temper. His father gave him a bag of nails and told him that every time he lost his temper, to hammer a nail in the back fence. The first day, the boy had driven 37 nails into the fence. Then it gradually dwindled down. He discovered it was easier to hold his temper than to drive those nails into the fence. Finally, the day came when the boy didn't lose his temper at all.*

*He told his father about it and the father then suggested that the boy now pull out one nail for each day that he was able to hold his temper. The days passed by and the young boy was finally able to tell his father that all the nails were gone.*

*The father took his son by the hand and led him to the fence. He said, 'You have done well, my son, but look at the holes in the fence. The fence will never be the same. When you say things in anger, they leave a scar just like this one. You can put a knife in a man and draw it out. It won't matter how many times you say, 'I am sorry', the wound is still there. A verbal wound is as bad as a physical one.'*

How many times do we say things in anger and haste, not realizing that we can never undo the ill-effects and hurt caused by our attitude? How often do we talk about people behind their backs believing that it's okay? Do we realize that even our thoughts of anger, though not heard by anybody, are causing damage to our own selves?

Anger is an emotion we can all identify with, both in terms of feeling it ourselves and identifying it in other people. However, it's also an emotion about which we are often confused about, because we are not very clear what we are supposed to do with anger.

Some get away with anger by saying, 'It's only human.' But are they aware that this approach will never solve their problem?

## WHAT REALLY IS ANGER?

Anger is nothing but a defense of the ego...defense against fear of being humiliated or embarrassed, fear of being minimized, fear of being mocked, fear of loss and of losing face...basically a FEAR OF LOSING. Put another way, *fear of not getting our way.*

Our ego always encourages us to win (even if we are incorrect) and when we are unable to get our way, our ego is hurt and it lashes out with the sword of anger solely to prove dominance. Over the years we have been wrongly taught that angry people are strong. *However, anger is, in fact, a direct proof of weakness.* Anyone who is acting in a destructive or aggressive way towards other people is actually a person who lacks inner harmony.

When one is full of turmoil within, that is what one will give out. On the other hand, a person displaying gentleness is the really happy soul who has true strength and inner harmony.

## WHAT IGNITES ANGER?

Each of us has a set of rules or expectations based on which we judge things to be right or wrong. Anger normally ignites when any important 'rule' of our life has been violated by someone. So, *anger is mainly rooted in judgement.* If someone does not meet our expectation, we get angry.

Worse still, if anger is not controlled, it starts a roller coaster ride with no terminal destination. What results? Complete chaos and unhappiness which puts the frame of mind into a state of revenge and retaliation.

When we are angry, we create damaging chemicals in our body that adversely affect our stomach lining, our blood pressure, our endocrine glands, our immune system, and so on. In addition, anger only gets in the way of effective action.

Further, anger encourages us to cause violence, wars and incredible heartache. Anger destroys us from the inside out (by our chemical secretions) or from the outside in (by the bullet of an enemy). But being aware of the disastrous results of anger does not stop us, a stubborn species of conditioning, in persisting on holding onto anger despite the physical and emotional consequences.

To add fuel to fire, our media projects angry people as 'heroes' for us. All the Rambos and Dirty Harrys portray anger in the righteous way. They convey that if you are being wronged, it is acceptable to be furious and even to kill. This portrayal is a great disservice to us because if we want to be happy, anger should be avoided and not encouraged.

## HOW TO CONTROL ANGER?

When you are angry you normally feel that others have *hurt your feelings*? Actually, they have done nothing to you. They are simply acting in the way they choose to act. You are the one who chooses to re-act with hurt, anger or whatever other e-motion (energy in motion) you choose.

Of course it's important to be assertive and have the confidence to confront people, if needed, but being emotionally involved to the point where we are jacked up, accompanied by high blood pressure and what not, is very counter productive, isn't it?

When an upsetting event occurs, just be patient because *DELAY is the antidote to anger.* Simply delay your response. And be aware that you are on the verge of getting angry. Then consciously choose a positive response rather than choosing anger and irritation. You can remind yourself – 'I don't have any right to expect perfection from everybody till I am perfect myself.' This will surely kill your emotion to react.

Once you realize that people are going to be exactly the way they are, irrespective of your opinion about them, you will allow yourself to simply BE in the relationship with everybody without any judgement, anger or hostility.

Knowing how to recognize and express anger appropriately will enable you to reach goals, handle emergencies, solve problems and even protect your health. Contrarily, failure to recognize and understand your anger may lead you to a variety of problems and unhappiness because anger can transform even the most beautiful person into a devil of insanity.

The choice is yours. Would you prefer the pain of anger which is like burning red-hot coals in your heart or would you rather accept everybody's imperfections and behaviours and respond with love? *Only love and understanding can dissolve anger.*

Once you expect others to be different, you will expect them to disagree with you. But knowing that they have a right to choose (just as you have that right) you will not choose to feel angry.

*Take a vow that you will get rid of the expectations you have for others. When the expectations go away so will your temper.* Remember that in spite of all your efforts, things will often happen that will make you angry and sometimes it is justifiable anger. Life will always be filled with frustration, pain, loss and unpredictable actions of others. You can't change that.

But you can change the way you let such events affect you. It is possible for you to feel anger but not necessarily behave in an angry way. This distinction between feelings and behaviours is the crucial step towards being free from losing self-control.

It's natural to get defensive when you are criticized or hurt without reason. At such instances, learn to hiss like a snake if necessary, but never learn to bite like it.

Go ahead then. Have your feelings, *but don't let your feelings have you.*

## THINK OF THE DAMAGE

*'I lose my temper, but it's all over in a minute,'*
*Said a student.*
*'So is the Hydrogen Bomb,' I replied,*
*'But think of the damage it produces!'*

—George Sweeting

Something soulful

## SPEAK GENTLY

Speak gently: it is better far
To rule by love than fear;
Speak gently: let not harsh words mar
The good we might do here.

Speak gently: love doth whisper low
The vows that true hearts bind;
And gently friendship's accents flow:
Affection's voice is kind.

Speak gently to the little child:
Its love be sure to gain;
Teach it in accents soft and mild:
It may not long remain.

Speak gently to the aged one;
Grieve not the careworn heart;
The sands of life are nearly run;
Let such in peace depart.

Speak gently to the young; for they
Will have enough to bear;
Pass through this life as best they may,
'Tis full of anxious care.

Speak gently, kindly, to the poor;
Let no harsh tone be heard:
They have enough they must endure,
Without an unkind word.

Speak gently to the erring; know
They may have toiled in vain;
Perchance unkindness made them so:
Oh, win them back again.

Speak gently: He who gave his life
To bend man's stubborn will,
When elements were in fierce strife,
Said to them, 'Peace, be still!'

Speak gently: 'tis a little thing
Dropped in the heart's deep well;
The good, the joy, which it may bring
Eternity shall tell.

—*Lewis J. Bates*

## Action plan

1) Anger can be kept under control if you are conscious and aware every moment of the day.

> Every morning when you wake up, confirm to yourself – *'Come what may I will choose to remain calm at least for this one day.'* See, the miraculous change in your level of peace and happiness if you stick to this task the whole day. Then you will feel the power of remaining calm.

2) Anger will almost always encourage the other person to continue to act as he has been. So instead of getting upset with anger, simply remember that the other person has a right to be different from what you would prefer him to be.

> Quietly tell yourself, 'If he wishes to behave foolishly or immaturely, *I am not going to get upset because he, not me, is behaving in that dumb way.'* Then simply respond to his immaturity as you would do to a child…with compassion.

*Young Student: 'Teacher, will you be angry at me for something I haven't done?'*
*Teacher: 'No, my child, never!'*
*Young Student: 'Well, madam, I haven't done my homework.'*

# 4

**Live Life Laughing**

## Inspiring thoughts

- We don't laugh because we are happy. We are happy because we laugh.

  —*William James*

- Laughter is an instant vacation.

  —*Milton Berle*

- When people are laughing, they're generally not killing each other.
  —*Alan Alda*

- Seven days without laughter makes one weak.

  —*Mort Walker*

- Laughter is an orgasm triggered by the intercourse of sense and nonsense.

  —*Author Unknown*

- Men show their character in nothing more clearly than by what they think laughable.

  —*Goethe*

- Nobody ever died of laughing.

  —*Max Beerbohm*

- Everybody laughs the same in every language because laughter is a universal connection.

  —*Yakov Smirnoff*

- Laughter is inner jogging.

  —*Norman Cousins*

- Laugh and the world laughs *with* you. Cry and the world laughs *at* you.

  —*Just* Win *Singh*

An Oriental proverb states – 'Time spent laughing is time spent with the Gods.' How true! When we are laughing, we are in a blissful state of mind and completely involved with life. Our worries are forgotten, our problems are forgotten…we are simply enjoying the moment.

Very few things in life are good for us and also fun; laughter is one such thing. But we human beings are a confused lot. We have an unnecessary habit of always taking for granted anything free of cost that makes us happy. We would rather pay a fee and then enjoy. That's the reason so few people even think it's worthwhile to laugh.

It's time, therefore, to bring to the forefront one of the most essential senses a human needs to develop – a sense of humour. Humour is the true index of happiness of any civilization. *The higher the level of humour, the happier the civilization.*

True humour is fun. It does not put down, mock or hurt anybody. It makes people feel wonderful, not separate, different and cut-off. True humour is based on the understanding that we are all in this together…that we are a Uni-Verse.

The ability to laugh at life's events is probably worth millions. *When we are faced with a problem, it is better to loosen up and face it as a challenge rather than as a tension.* And changing perspective is all that is required to do so. Even our instincts tell us that we need to laugh, to make life fun, to rid ourselves of stodgy thoughts and hardening of the attitudes specially during testing times.

Further, humour helps us in accepting our imperfections with ease. When we learn to laugh at our mishaps, we are able to instantaneously transform perceived bad situations into opportunities to learn something about the absurdity of human behaviour, particularly our own.

We encourage you now to give yourself permission to laugh. You will be amazed at how quickly a crisis can turn into a comedy when you invite in humour.

Wouldn't it be great to see everybody laughing and enjoying himself? Even our Creator would feel proud that his gift of life is being finally appreciated by one and all. If waves of laughter start sweeping the land, what chance will the waves of violence have?

The next time things are going crazy, remember:

*Don't tighten up; just lighten up!*

> *One can know a man from his laugh and if you like a man's laugh before you know anything of him, you may confidently say that he is a good man.*
> —Fyodor Dostoyevsky

Diane Johnson has made a beautiful statement – '*Laughter is the jam on the toast of life. It adds flavor, keeps it from being too dry, and makes it easier to swallow.*'

The good news is that this jam is readily available with each one of us, every minute of our lives with an inexhaustible stock. Mother Nature was extremely generous to let every individual have as much of this jam as he feels like using.

But have you noticed how stingy we are in using our laughter…as if our stock of fun may finish any day. So we save it for another day. Let me work hard today and enjoy and laugh later, you say!! But the golden question is – when will that day come?

The time is NOW, to live life, to enjoy life and to experience life to the fullest. And taking time out for laughter can be a wonderful way to unwind, relax and simply *be*. When we are laughing, we forget everything else. We are so connected with life, so alive and in the true sense — really living. And while laughing, we forget the past or future and are simply enjoying the present…which is the best way to utilize every moment, isn't it?

## IT'S JUST A MATTER OF PERSPECTIVE

Most people have been brought up in societies and environments that always talk of gloom and despair (no wonder newspapers sell so well). They have been living with the belief that life is supposed to be 'one hard road' and if you are enjoying yourself while travelling on it, something is drastically wrong with you and maybe you are crazy. But people who preach this are the ones who are the saddest in life. And never listen to such people. Since they did not have the guts to enjoy life, they cannot accept anybody enjoying it.

It is not true that life is a smooth road without problems. But how you look at life is the important difference which must be understood. Simply put, *life can be a serious matter or life can be a laughing matter. We can choose either perspective at any given time.* By laughing at the events of life, we tend to see things differently. This makes us feel differently and hence we behave differently. This changes our reality. So, laughter is often the catalyst that makes this good change in us possible.

It is, therefore, essential to practice developing our sense of humour just as we try to develop our other senses. A person without a sense of humour is like a wagon without springs that gets jolted by every pebble on the road of life.

When we laugh, we simply shift our perspective and the problems of our life shrink to a manageable size. Even though the problem may persist, laughter causes at least the misery to vanish. It teaches us to lighten up and take ourselves less seriously, even in the most serious situations.

## THE DIFFERENCE BETWEEN BEING 'CHILDISH' AND BEING 'CHILD-LIKE'

Human beings are not born serious. We begin life fully equipped with an innate playfulness and the ability to laugh freely (observe a child anytime). Sadly, we curb our playfulness and laughter to the serious business of adulthood. People actually shout at you and tell you to 'grow up'.

So, we consciously kill the child within us and start *behaving* like grown ups. Anytime you are playful or silly, everybody screams – 'Stop acting like a child.'

Somewhere, over the years, something has gone drastically wrong while human beings became more cultured and so-called society folk. Instead of being taught the message of growing up and still remaining child-like, our playfulness and laughter has been labeled 'childish'. The difference is quite clear yet not conveyed from generation to generation effectively.

A *childish* person is an adult who still has the characteristics of a child. If you still cry for your needs, or fight at petty matters, or break the discipline needed for your growth in life, etc., you can be termed as childish.

If, however, you are an adult with well-developed faculties to reason with life correctly and yet you still have the playfulness of a child, then you can be termed as *child-like*. Unfortunately, since childish behaviour can be damaging to an adult's progress, and since the difference between being childish and being child-like has never been made crystal clear to most individuals, we prefer to put up a show of maturity by being serious. Before we know it, we have mastered the art of being serious and then we don't know how to release the safety valve when the pressure and stress of a hectic life takes its toll on us.

To make things worse, in our frenzy to succeed and have it all, we have shortened everything. We have fast food, fast banking, fast shopping and even fast sex...imagine! So, laughter is completely ruled out of our system *because you cannot hurry laughter*. It has to be enjoyed by being in the moment and not rushing here and there. This is one of the major reasons why so few people have the time to laugh.

## WHY DEVELOP THE HABIT OF LAUGHING?

When Nature designed our bodies, it did not provide us with a sense of humour just for grins. *It included it as a built-in safety valve to deal with stress.* Laughter is that safety valve, which once opened, allows us to release our tension, by giving us an internal massage.

If you have truly ever laughed, you would have noticed that there is something about laughter and a sense of humour that is extremely healing. Laughter is our body's way of giving us a break from anxiety, frustration and irritation.

While we take really good care of our health, are we ever aware that absence of illness is not health; *true health is JOY!* Health professionals are becoming increasingly aware that health, wholeness, humour and happiness are interrelated. And the easiest way to keep living joyfully is to never lose the 'silliness' of the child you were.

## TRY BEING SILLY

The word *silly* is derived from two old European words: *seely* and *saelig*, both of which mean 'blessed', 'happy' and 'joyful'. Children enjoy being silly; adults rarely understand. Children are natural comedians looking for endless possibilities of nonsense, absurdity and silliness.

One of the most important functions of silliness is that the act of being silly helps us to keep the mind young, fresh, alive and relatively unconditioned. So, we tend to be more creative to handle every situation of life, whether good or bad.

Silliness also serves to calm, pacify and control the ego. The ability to laugh at yourself is another serious and vital function of silliness. To be able to laugh at oneself indicates a healthy self-respect, confidence, and a high degree of inner comfort. And we all know, it is easy to be comfortable with people who are comfortable with themselves. Now you know why you feel absolutely relaxed in the company of happy, laughing souls.

From today, instead of running away from life, laugh right at its face and see how you start enjoying yourself.

Start living the way you want to (...you have just got the permission to be silly). Live life straight from the heart. Do what makes you happy. Laugh whenever you feel like. Enjoy every minute (it may be your last) and always spread sunshine everywhere you go.

*Remember, what goes on around you need not determine what goes on inside you.* This is one of the most important secrets of joyful living.

So, keep laughing, keep loving, keep living and be truly silly!

## *LAUGH WITH LIFE, NOT AT IT*

*Some people choose to laugh at life rather than laugh with it.*
*Laughing* at *is defensive, devisory and divisive;*
*Laughing* with *helps us to be comfortable, to connect and to bond.*
*Happy confident people tend to laugh with;*
*Unhappy, unconfident people tend to resort to laughing at.*
*Which one are you?*

—*Author Unknown*

## WHY DON'T YOU LAUGH?

Why don't you laugh, young man, when troubles come,
Instead of sitting around so sour and glum?
You cannot have all play,
And sunshine every day;
When troubles come,
Why don't you laugh?

Why don't you laugh? It will ever help to soothe
The aches and pains. No road is smooth;
There's many an unseen bump,
And many a hidden stump,
Over which you'll have to jump.
Why don't you laugh?

Why don't you laugh? Don't let your spirits wilt;
Don't sit and cry because the milk you've spilt;
If you could mend it now,
Pray let me tell you how:
Just milk another cow!
Why don't you laugh?

Why don't you laugh, and make us all laugh, too,
And keep us mortals all from getting blue?
A laugh will always win;
If you can't laugh, just grin –
Come on, let's all join in!
Why don't you laugh?

—*The Independent*

## IT'S UP TO YOU!

Laugh a little, sing a little, as you go your way!
Work a little, play a little, do this every day!
Give a little, take a little, never mind a frown!
Make your smile a welcome thing, all around the town!
Laugh a little, love a little, skies are always blue!
Every cloud has silver linings, but it's up to you!

—*Author Unknown*

## Action plan

1) Make a conscious effort to laugh more often. Don't let a day go by when you fail to laugh heartily.

> *Take a smile time-out.* Take a deep breath, smile, exhale and say 'Aaah!' while visualizing all your muscles and cells of your body smiling. Then add to that a memory of a time you felt really good and laughed and laughed. See how good you start feeling instantaneously.

2) Treat yourself to some fun today. Remember, it's now or never.

> *Do something that you love doing.* Don't delay it. Feel the pleasure of doing what you want to do, NOW!! Once you do what you love, you will automatically be thankful to life for letting you enjoy the pleasure of doing something you enjoy doing. With that frame of mind, you will be more ready to laugh and enjoy the other events of your life, which you may have otherwise perceived to be disastrous.

*A good wife laughs at her husband's jokes,*
*not because they are clever,*
*but because she is.*

# 5

## Why Worry?

## Inspiring thoughts

- Don't worry about the world ending today. It's already tomorrow in Australia.

    —*Charles Schulz*

- Worrying is like a rocking chair. It gives you something to do but doesn't get you anywhere.

    —*Dorothy Galyean*

- My life is filled with terrible misfortune, most of which never happened.

    —*Michel De Montaigne*

- Worry does not empty tomorrow of its sorrow. It empties today of its strength.

    —*Corrie Ten Boom*

- Blessed is the person who is too busy to worry in the daytime and too sleepy to worry at night.

    —*Author Unknown*

- Don't take tomorrow to bed with you.

    —*Norman Vincent Peale*

- Worry is the dark room in which negatives are developed.

    —*Author Unknown*

- The reason why worry kills more people than work is that more people worry than work.

    —*Robert Frost*

- We have a past TENSE, a present TENSE and a future TENSE. So when can we be happy?

    —*Just* Win *Singh*

The present period in History is being rightly called the *Age of Anxiety.* The problem of worry has become one of the most common struggles of modern man. And it is growing like a cancer.

Worry is just about the worst form of mental activity (other that hate) which is extremely self-destructive and a strong cause of unhappiness. Worry keeps us focused in the past or the future and robs the present moment of its joy.

Most people confuse worrying with planning for the future. Planning for a great future is necessary and it implies that you are concentrating on doing every thing you can today to ensure a tomorrow the way you want it to be. Whereas worrying implies that you do nothing but get immobilized with fear of the possible outcome. You just sit back and keep thinking of all the demons of destruction who are waiting to get you, and that makes you endlessly shake your legs while sitting on the sofa.

*If we carefully observe, we will agree that about ninety percent of the things in our lives are right and only about ten percent are wrong.* Unfortunately, the bug of perfection that has been inserted in us since childhood makes us focus and try to correct the ten percent that are wrong. And while doing so, we miss out the fun we could have had by appreciating and enjoying the ninety percent that is right. If you want to be happy, all you have to do is concentrate on the ninety percent of life that is right and ignore the ten percent that is wrong.

If that is too difficult for you, here is a diagonally opposite observation:

40% of the things we worry about will never happen

30% concern old decisions which cannot be altered

12% centre in criticisms, mostly untrue, made by people who feel inferior

10% is related to our health, which worsens while we worry.

8% is legitimate, showing that life does have real problems which may be met head on when we have eliminated senseless worries.

So, instead of going around cursing life for its miseries, and getting crushed under the burden of accumulated yesterdays and fearful tomorrows, start taking charge of your life with the motto – *Do your best and leave the rest.*

For, if you know you have done your best, what else is left to be done?

> *Happy the man, and happy he alone;*
> *he, who can call today his own;*
> *He who, secure within, can say:*
> *'Tomorrow, do thy worst,*
> *for I have lived today.'*
> —Horace

## STORY-TIME

*There was a Chinese widow whose sole means of support was her two sons. The older son sold umbrellas while the younger son sold sunglasses. The woman worried every single day because when it was sunny, the older son wouldn't sell any umbrellas. If it were raining, the younger son wouldn't sell any sunglasses. So, no matter what the weather, she worried...and worried...and worried.*

*One day a wise, old friend dropped by for a visit. The friend was alarmed at how thin and pale the widow had become. 'Are you ill, my dear?' asked the friend. 'No,' replied the widow, 'I'm just worried all the time. No matter what the weather, one of my sons will not make any sales for the day.'*

*The wise old friend smiled and said, 'Oh, no, my friend. You, of all people, shouldn't have a worry in the world, for you can't help but win. For you see, no matter what the weather, one of your sons will always sell his wares.'*

Life is nothing but a matter of perspective, a matter of how you look at it. How often have you worried about something, only to find out that everything turned out fine in the end? What did the worry get you except headaches and loss of sleep?

## WHAT IS 'WORRY'?

*Worry is nothing but a misuse of our imagination.* It is a spasm of emotions in which the mind takes hold of a thought and clutches to it spasmodically.

The word 'Worry' is derived from an Anglo-Saxon word meaning *to strangle* or *to choke*. The ancient Saxons compared worry to a vicious animal clutching at a man's throat. No wonder when we are worried, we feel as if something is clutching our throat and that we may literally choke to death.

When someone says 'I'm worried to death' or 'I am sick with worry' he is not very far from the truth because worry can definitely make you sick and has even been a known cause for death. Our hospitals and cemeteries are full of people who made worry their everyday companion and became *mental lepers* as their minds were eaten away by negative thoughts.

If you are like a lot of people, worry just might be one of the things that makes life miserable for you by making you lose sleep, drop weight, develop nervous tics or make you suffer from gastric disorders, ulcers, etc.

One of the worst features of worry is that it destroys our ability to concentrate. When worried, we are in a state of mental chaos and our mind jumps here and there making us lose all our power of decision making.

We get so stuck up in something we are worried about that may happen in the future, that we absolutely forget to live in the present.

## WHY DO PEOPLE WORRY?

Most people have been brought up with the conditioning that we must first SECURE our future and then enjoy. Haven't you been told that, too? Well, stop everything, pick up a pen and write down how many people do you know who actually sit back, arms folded over their heads, lazily enjoying themselves on a Monday morning, saying 'I don't need to work any more...my future is secure.' Start...

What happened? You couldn't write anybody's name? Why? When generations of parents have been teaching us to secure ourselves, how is it that not one of us can confidently sit back and say I AM SECURE?

It is because *security is a myth.* Nobody can ever secure his future because there are so many unforeseen possibilities attached to the future. That is the reason why all the great people have always been preaching the value of living in the present. Because no human being can really know what the future has in store for him/her. So, why lose precious present moments worrying about a future which we cannot control?

No doubt adult life brings certain responsibilities which are inescapable facts of maturity (and a direct proof that the world needs us) but no matter what or how heavy our duties, why not retain a happy and youthful spirit rather than getting immobilized by worry?

Urging you to leave your worry behind, does not imply that you should be indifferent to human suffering or carelessly disregard your own problems or the problems of your society. We need to be concerned about our problems, but not worried.

## THE DIFFERENCE BETWEEN CONCERN & WORRY

Eliminating worry does not mean that you should stop being concerned as many may interpret. There is a difference between worry and concern. Concern means realizing what the problems are and CALMLY taking steps to meet them. Worrying means going around in maddening, futile circles.

*A worried person SEES a problem. A concerned person SOLVES a problem.* It is as simple as that. Ask yourself, do you just see a problem and worry or do you sincerely put efforts to find a solution to it?

Most worriers are either simply lazy people or people who lack self-confidence to take up the challenges of life. Such people *choose* to worry since it's easier to sit back and worry rather than do something about the situation.

## HOW TO ELIMINATE WORRY?

Do you know how many people beat themselves up over things they are unable to change? On the other hand, do you know how many people waste time worrying about things they really could change?

Isn't it ironical? Much of our worry concerns things over which we have no control. You can worry all you want about the economy, war, possible illness, etc. but worry won't bring you prosperity, peace or health. Worry is a chain reaction which transmits a negative vibration, through your attitude, to the minds of all who are in your presence, and before you know it, everybody is feeling down.

Here is how to stop your habit of worrying. It makes no sense to worry about those things over which you believe you have no control. And it also makes no sense to worry about the things over which you have control, because if you have control over them, then there is no reason to worry.

The next time you catch yourself worrying, immediately get a grip. Try to figure out if you can do something about it or not. If so, then go ahead and do. If not, then try changing yourself first, by developing new abilities, and then attacking the problem. Either way, worry isn't the answer.

And stop worrying about the future. Stop wasting these precious present moments on behaviour that has absolutely no positive pay off for you. No living man can possibly figure out what is going to happen in future because there are so many forces that will affect your future apart from what you worry for. So what's the point?

Remember, our peace of mind and the joy we get out of living depends not on where we are, or what we have, or who we are, but solely upon *how we look at life*. If your attitude is correct you can blossom like a lotus in the murky pond of life.

There is nothing to be worried about! Absolutely nothing! You can either do something about a situation or you can spend the rest of your life, worrying. But get this clear in your mind...*no amount of your worry will ever change a thing.*

### NEVER MIND IT

*For every ailment under the sun,*
*There is a remedy, or there is none.*
*If there be one, try to find it;*
*If there be none, never mind it.*

—*Mother Goose Rhyme*

( *Something soulful* )

## TWO DAYS WE SHOULD NOT WORRY

There are two days in every week about which we should
not worry, two days which should be kept free from fear and
apprehension.

One of these days is Yesterday with all its mistakes and cares,
its faults and blunders, its aches and pains.

Yesterday has passed forever beyond our control.
All the money in the world cannot bring back Yesterday.

We cannot undo a single act we performed;
we cannot erase a single word we said.
Yesterday is gone forever.

The other day we should not worry about is Tomorrow
with all its possible adversities, its burdens,
its large promise and its poor performance;
Tomorrow is also beyond our immediate control.

Tomorrow's sun will rise,
either in splendour or behind a mask of clouds, but it will rise.
Until it does, we have no stake in Tomorrow,
for it is yet to be born.

This leaves only one day, Today.
Any person can fight the battle of just one day.
It is when you and I add the burdens of those two awful eternities
Yesterday and Tomorrow that we break down.

It is not the experience of Today that drives a person mad,
it is the remorse or bitterness of something which happened
Yesterday and the dread of what Tomorrow may bring.

Let us, therefore, live but one day at a time.

—*Author Unknown*

## UNLESS YOU LET THEM IN

All the water in the world, however hard it tried,
Could never, never sink a ship, unless it got inside.
All the hardships of this world, might wear you pretty thin,
But they won't hurt you one least bit…
Unless you let them in.

—*Author Unknown*

## Action plan

1) Do what Winston Churchill suggested.

> *Write down six things that are worrying you.* Two of them will, say, disappear while you write. About two of them, probably nothing can be done, so it's no use worrying. And the remaining two can, perhaps be settled with proper action.

2) Try to think everyday, how you can please someone.

> We worry because we have the time to think of ourselves. The moment you catch yourself feeling worried, *immediately go ahead and do a good deed for someone.* (one that brings a smile of joy on the face of another.) This will not only cause you to stop thinking of yourself, it will make you feel happier for simply adding a ray of joy to somebody else's life.

*The assistant manager, noticing the frown on his superior's face, said, "You sure look worried!"*
*'Listen,' replied the manager, 'I have so many worries that if something happens today, I won't have time to worry about if for another two weeks.'*

# 6
## Become Fearless

## Inspiring thoughts

- One can attain a high degree of security in a prison cell if that's all he wants out of life.

  —*Dwight Eisenhower*

- Nothing in life is to be feared. It is only to be understood.

  —*Marie Curie*

- Courage is not the absence of fear; it is the conquest of it.

  —*Author unknown*

- Keep your fears to yourself but share your courage with others.

  —*Robert Louis Stevenson*

- Don't be afraid your life will end. Be afraid it will never begin.

  —*Grace Hansen*

- Fear is that little darkroom where negatives are developed.

  —*Michael Pritchard*

- You block your dream when you allow your fear to grow bigger than your faith.

  —*Mary Manin Morrissey*

- I believe that every single event in life happens as an opportunity to choose love over fear.

  —*Oprah Winfrey*

- Fear is a feeling created by our body when it wants to tell us – 'Don't just sit there, do something!'

  —*Just* Win *Singh*

We were given every emotion for a reason. The purpose of natural fear is to build in us a bit of caution to help keep our body alive. So, fear, in the true sense, is merely an outgrowth of love…love for self.

Though this emotion was given by Nature to protect us, we have gotten so scared by it in life, that now fear controls most of us. And falling into the hands of fear puts us in a vicious cycle since fear breeds inaction…inaction leads to inexperience…inexperience generates inability…and inability creates fear.

In one way or another, fear prevents people from getting what they want in life. Fear is the greatest single obstacle to success. And the basic seed of fear is INDECISION. *Indecision crystallizes into doubt and the two blend and become fear.*

Too often, people let their fear rule over their decisions and actions. They yearn for nothing but security. And since security is a myth, they can never get their hold on it. So, they keep trying to achieve the impossible and this keeps them in the mode of unhappiness.

There is only one way to fully experience this gift of life. Only when you can answer all your 'what ifs' with 'I can handle it,' can you approach all things with a no-lose guarantee. Only then can you become fearless.

From this moment start thinking of yourself as a lifetime student at the University of Life and instead of sitting home like a victim of your insecurities, reach out into the world and see that LIFE REALLY IS BEAUTIFUL.

Develop a trust in whatever life wants you to experience. Remember, the forces of the creator are always with you.

*No soul can be forever banned*
*Eternally bereft;*
*Whoever falls from God's right hand*
*Is caught into his left. (Edwin Markham)*

Only when you have absolute faith that everything happens to you to enable you to experience more in life, only then will you start flowing with life (instead of trying to beat it) and once you are free from being caught up with the fear of consequences, you will no longer be afraid of anything.

Only then will you really begin to live.

> *Never fear shadows. They simply mean there's a light shining somewhere nearby.*
> —Ruth E. Renkel

## STORY-TIME

*The Golden Gate Bridge is the highest and longest single span bridge in the world. There is a mile of it hanging over the bay at San Francisco. When it was being built, the bridge was so high, it looked down from its great height into the black waters so far below that the men who were building it – even though they were experienced bridge builders – felt a terrible fear.*

*The bridge cost thirty five million dollars. There was a superstition among builders that for every million dollars spent on the bridge, a human life must be sacrificed. This had already cost the lives of five men on the Golden Gate Bridge, although every safety device was used. Men were ordered to wear steel helmets, rubber shoes, iron girder grippers and every safety device known to science.*

*Yet still they fell. It was FEAR that was pushing them off the bridge just as certainly as if it stood behind them as they worked. One day it was decided to put a safety net under the bridge. This was a net woven of steel strands like a large fish net. It was put under the bridge and swung from one end to the other. If any worker fell off the bridge, he fell into the net and could be hauled back to safety.*

*Now the bridge was as high as before, the girders just as slippery, the water just as black and far below. But a wonderful thing happened. From that time on not a single man fell off the bridge into the net!*

*Why? Because they were no longer afraid. And they were no longer afraid because they realized that even if they did fall, the safety net was there to catch them. When they lost their fear of falling, they did not fall.*

What's the moral of the story? If you safety net (faith in yourself / life) is missing, you will tend to become fearful. Let's see how we can get the safety net back into position to make you fearless. For that it is important to understand what exactly is – fear.

## WHAT IS 'FEAR'?

*Fear is nothing but WORRY MAGNIFIED.* It is a state of mind in which we have a lack of belief in ourselves and we somehow lose confidence in our ability to handle any kind of situation life makes us face.

All of us suffer from fear. Fear is an emotion intended to help preserve our lives by warning us of some forthcoming danger. Hence, fear can be a blessing when it raises its flag of caution, causing us to pause and study a particular situation before making a decision or taking action. Once it has served its purpose as a warning signal, we have to be careful not to permit it to enter into the logical reasoning by which we decide to take a certain course of action.

Unfortunately for us, we are unable to draw the fine line where we must feel the fear and then control it before it has a chance to control us. Do you know why we get stuck up with the pangs of fear?

One of the major reasons is that our society has brought us up with a foolish logic – 'In order to be good enough, we have to be perfect.' Now since nobody is perfect, it implies that nobody is good enough...and that's what makes us lose our confidence in ourselves. That's what develops our fearful nature.

It is so amazing that though mistakes (imperfections) are an integral part of learning in the process of living, we have been taught that we must be 'perfect.' This ironical 'mistake' in our thinking, has created a fearful mindset in everybody.

Because of this background of fear (since childhood) *we get into the habit of anticipating the worst.* We begin to assume that negative thinking is more realistic and being positive is unrealistic. And since we are feeding ourselves with negatives, we act and ensure that they become our reality.

Our lack of confidence leads us to think negative thoughts which produce needless wear and tear of our mental motors. Before we know it we are making mental monsters out of almost any unpleasant happening. Our fearful nature explains why we still have economic recessions. Fear explains why millions of people accomplish little and enjoy little. The lives of thousands of families are mutilated and often ruined by this bugbear of misfortune just ahead.

## HOW TO BECOME FEARLESS?

You will agree that at the bottom of every one of your fears is simply the fear that you can't handle whatever life will bring you, isn't it? If you somehow KNEW that you could handle anything that came your way, what would you possibly have to fear? The answer is – NOTHING!

Now the only way to diminish your fear is for you to develop more trust in your ability to handle whatever comes your way. That ability will develop once you MAKE LIFE A GAME and try to *play it instead of fight it.*

Take every event as a new adventure in life and keep the attitude – 'It will be interesting to see what happens.' This way you will be open to any consequence of your action and no matter where life takes you, you will be in a no-lose situation because you are now focused on enjoying the experience rather that achieving a result. So, which ever way life will take you, you will be ready to go and before you know it, you will start 'handling' whatever comes your way.

Every encounter that forces you to 'handle it' will raise your self-esteem considerably. As you keep feeling the fear and doing it anyway, you will slowly develop a trust in yourself that no matter what, you will survive.

## TAKE ACTION

Dale Carnegie made a very true statement – 'Inaction breeds doubt and fear. Action breeds confidence and courage. If you want to conquer fear, do not sit home and think about it. Go out and get busy.'

One of the biggest fear that keeps us from moving ahead with our lives is our difficulty in making decisions. However, do we realize that even by not choosing, we ARE choosing! We are choosing to deprive ourselves of what makes life a delicious feast.

So, go ahead and take action. If you get what you wanted, you will have killed your fear. If you don't get what you want, you can go ahead and try another option. Both ways you will have a life experience you would have otherwise missed had you just sat home. And life is nothing but an 'experience.'

Anyone who has 'handled' the death of a loved one, the loss of a job, illness, divorce, etc. has definitely emerged a much stronger person who will have discovered that *security is not having things; it's handling things.*

Go ahead then and 'handle' life the way it comes. If you can create your own misery, then by the same logic, you should also be able to create your own joy. So what's stopping you?

Start developing the inner knowing that you can handle anything life hands you and soon you will start *enjoying* the mysteries of life instead of feeling *threatened* by them. Remember, you have only one life to live. Make the most of it. Take the good and bad experiences with equal acceptance.

The game of life is a lot like football. You have to *tackle* your problems, *block* your fears and *score* your points when you get the opportunity. So to succeed in life, learn to prepare for the worst, expect the best and take what comes.

Go ahead then and *happily achieve rather than achieve to be happy.*

## NO HEAVENLY FATHER

*Said the Robin to the Sparrow: 'I should really like to know*
*Why these anxious human beings rush about and worry so.'*
*Said the Sparrow to the Robin: 'Friend, I think it must be*
*That they have no heavenly Father such as cares for you and me.'*

—Elizabeth Cheney

*Something soulful*

## THE COMFORT ZONE

I used to have a comfort zone where I knew I wouldn't fail.

The same four walls and busywork were really more like jail.
I longed so much to do the things I'd never done before,
But stayed inside my comfort zone and paced the same old floor.

I said it didn't matter that I wasn't doing much.
I said I didn't care for things like commission cheques and such.
I claimed to be so busy with the things inside the zone,
But deep inside I longed for something special of my own.

I couldn't let my life go by just watching others win.
I held my breath; I stepped outside and let the change begin.
I took a step and with new strength I'd never felt before,
I kissed my comfort zone goodbye and closed and locked the door.

If you're in a comfort zone, afraid to venture out,
Remember that all winners were at one time filled with doubt.
A step or two and words of praise can make your dreams come true.
Reach for your future with a smile; Success is there for you!

—*Author Unknown*

## OUR DEEPEST FEAR

Our deepest fear is not that we are inadequate.
Our deepest fear is that we are powerful beyond measure.
It is our light, not our darkness, that most frightens us.
We ask ourselves, who am I to be brilliant, gorgeous, talented,
and fabulous?
Actually, who are you not to be? You are a child of God.
Your playing small doesn't serve the world.
There is nothing enlightened about shrinking so that
Other people won't feel insecure around you.
We are born to make manifest the Glory of God that is within us.
It's not just in some of us, it's in everyone,
And as we let our light shine,
We unconsciously give other people permission to do the same.
As we are liberated from our own fear,
Our presence automatically liberates others.

—*Nelson Mandela*

## Action plan

1) Isolate your fear. Pin it down and determine exactly what you are afraid of. Then take ACTION.

> *Action cures fear.* If you fear making a phone call you know you must make, then just pick up the phone and make the call NOW. If you make the call, the fear will disappear. If you, however, put it off, it will get harder and harder to make that call. Likewise, whatever you dread, just go ahead and do it before the fear freezes you into inaction.

2) Always do what is right. Doing what is right keeps your conscience satisfied and this builds self-confidence.

> When you do what you know is wrong, you not only feel guilty (which eats away your confidence) but you fear that sooner or later people will find out and lose confidence in you. *So why do something which hurts your conscience in the first place!*

*Pilot over the intercom: 'We have lost one of our engines. No need to worry, we will be arriving 1 hour later than anticipated.'*

*Pilot 30 minutes later: 'We have lost another engine so we will be arriving 2 hours later at our destination.'*

*Pilot one hour later: 'We have lost our third engine, too. We will, therefore, be arriving 4 hours late at our destination.'*

*Passenger to her husband: 'I'm starting to fear, if that last engine goes, we will be up here all night.'*

# 7

# There's No Such
# Thing as Failure

## Inspiring thoughts

- You are not a failure if you didn't make it. You are a success because you tried.

  *—Author Unknown*

- Failure is the line of least resistance.

  *—W A Clarke*

- Success is going from failure to failure without a loss of enthusiasm.

  *—Winston Churchill*

- Mountaintops inspire leaders but valleys mature them.

  *—J Philip Everson*

- I don't know the key to success, but the key to failure is trying to please everybody.

  *—Bill Cosby*

- This thing we call failure is not falling down, but staying down.

  *—Mary Pickford*

- If you try to fail and succeed, which have you done?

  *—Author Unknown*

- Remember that failure is an event, not a person.

  *—Zig Ziglar*

- I honestly think it is better to be a failure at something you love than to be a success at something you hate.

  *—Geroge Burns*

- All failures in life have success stories they may have made true.

  *—Just Win Singh*

Did you know that an electric bulb will follow the line of least resistance, but a bulb glows precisely because there *is* resistance?

Then why do we fear any setbacks which act as *resistance* in our plans to achieve a specific goal? Why don't we realize that the very resistance is going to provide us with the 'glow' we are chasing in our life?

In our superfast, need-more, gotta-get-it world, many people live with chronic anxiety and fear that they are not successful *enough* or they have failed. This happens became we are influenced by materialistic modes of success measurement, and are often confused and hoping that we, too, can prove ourselves to be successful in the eyes of the society as Mr. XYZ.

However, the real irony is that the person whose apparent success you covet may just be killing himself from the stress of pursuing goals that mean nothing to him...but that never enters your mind! This is a critical flaw in our wonderfully abundant culture – to assume someone is happy and successful just because he has specific tokens of accomplishments.

But for anybody to feel truly happy, he must be very clear about one thing – 'Happiness is as individual as our finger prints.' All we need is the courage to be ourselves and to do what we want (and not what the society says) in order to feel successful.

It is time to blast the myth of failure and encourage you to start living with the *principle of not how much, but how well*. Keep doing the thing you want to, fall down a hundred times, change your route map if needed, and keep learning from every event. *Judge your success not so much by the results as by the effort.* This is the only way to experience a full life and feel happily successful.

If you fail in a task, you need to simply keep moving on, hopefully a little humbler, wiser and more charitable as a result of the experience. Success must not be measured by what a man accomplishes but by the opposition he has encountered and the courage with which he has maintained the struggle against overwhelming odds.

So, whenever you are faced with a setback, never choose to sit back. Because the Lord gave you two ends, one for sitting and one for thinking. Your success depends on which one you use.

*Heads you win, Tails you lose.*

> Believe it or not:
> *Henry Ford forgot to put the reverse*
> *gear in the first car he made.*
> *Do you consider him a failure?*

A great researcher, having failed two hundred times before he found the answer to one of his burning questions was asked, 'Doesn't it bother you that you failed all those times?' His answer was, 'I never failed! I discovered two hundred ways how not to do something.'

Life is simply how we look at it. When we come out of the womb, we don't know how to walk or talk. Then as we grow we try to take our first few steps. Are we criticized for falling down when we begin to walk? No. In fact, we are cheered with big hugs, encouraged to try again. After innumerable tumbles, we are soon up and running everywhere.

Now, can you find one baby who felt that he should have known better and learnt faster how to walk? Can you locate one baby who, after a series of falls, decided never to try to walk again? Every single normal child finally learns to walk. And he does so because the child does what he does and he does so when it was supposed to be done. That is exactly how it works best for all of us in life.

Nature is wise enough to understand that unless you tumble and fall as a child, you will not be able to develop the strength in the muscles of your legs to enable you to walk properly. So, you keep falling until you learn. This part of Nature is universally accepted by everybody as normal.

As you grow into a man, you face more and more challenges and opportunities for growth both physically and intellectually. However, instead of accepting your setbacks as similar tumbles for your further growth, you slowly start labeling yourself as a failure. Now, why does this happen?

*It is because as a child you never had any expectations of the results of any of your actions.* But once you have grown up, you are attached to the result with a certain level of performance which you refer to in your mind as 'success.' And if you do not live up to that level (for whatever reason) your ego gets a whack and that's why you start feeling like a loser.

## WHY DO WE FEEL LIKE FAILURES?

Many parents, teachers, business supervisors, religious authorities and critics of all sorts are responsible for dulling our aspirations and destroying our dreams. 'Mistakes' are proclaimed as failures and subsequently we are punished.

Such an approach of our influencers leaves us afraid to take any further risks. So, we simply start analyzing every single action prior to doing something about it. And our fear gets stronger as we *give it more thought* and soon we are stuck with *analysis paralysis.*

This attitude prevents us from 'doing something' in order to succeed and instead we sit back and keep analyzing every possibility so as to ensure we do the thing perfectly and there is no chance of failure. This leads to inaction on our part and since we do nothing much to succeed, we often do not achieve the desired results. So, we feel like failures.

## THE CONCEPT OF FAILURE

You may be surprised to read this, but FAILURE DOES NOT EXIST. Failure is a judgment we humans place on a given action. Failure is simply someone else's opinion of how a certain act should be done. Your concept of failure comes from *believing someone else's opinion* about how you should hit the golf ball.

Once you believe that no act must be performed in any specific way OTHERS have decided, then failing becomes impossible. Events are merely events, in themselves, neither good nor bad. It is your attitude towards them which defines them so.

When you feel that you have failed in some event, instead of crying over the issue, get encouraged by your failure and try improving and planning better in future. *Failure will help you in revealing your weaknesses* so that you don't develop a false confidence by an easy success.

If you react to your negative feelings aggressively and positively, they can become challenges which automatically arouse more power and more ability within you. It all depends upon the individual and his attitudes, whether negative feelings are used as assets or liabilities.

Remember, it is not what happens to you that matters. It is how you see it that counts. *Failure should be your teacher, not your undertaker.* It should be a temporary detour and not a dead-end street.

If you can wake up to the fact that mistakes are simply feedback on how you are doing, you will finally emerge a winner. It is a known fact that winners make far more mistakes than losers. That's why they are winners...because they are getting more feedback as they continue to try more possibilities.

## CHANGE YOUR GAME PLAN

*Start expecting life to be great.* Always use your failure as a stepping stone to your success. And look at the good side of each situation. Just by changing your game plan, you will change the way you live and enjoy this life.

The next time your favourite cricket player misses an easy shot, cheer him instead of cursing him. If your child scores less marks in the exams, find out what part he did well, no matter how slight, and start building from there. Stop directly telling him about his mistakes. Instead, encourage him to simply keep trying and learning from each event.

If you can just understand that *to try is to succeed*, to give your best is what it's all about, then you will be far more peaceful with what results you achieve.

The easiest thing to do when you fail is to put yourself down by blaming your lack of ability for your misfortunes. With so many obstacles and hindrances, the average man and woman would be tempted to withdraw. But remember, you are far above average (otherwise you wouldn't be reading this) and you are made for greater things.

Start focusing your attention and effort to acquire the necessary knowledge, know-how and motivation to become an expert and achieve your specific desired objective. And while you are doing so, life will keep teaching you that you have as much strength in times of failure as in times of success.

Your setback becomes a great blessing if it leaves you gifted with humility of the heart and gratitude for those riches you still possess. In fact, *most of your failures and defeats are blessings in disguise as they force you to change your course in life so that you are led to greater opportunities, greater happiness and greater understanding.*

Don't wait for all the lights to become green before you leave for your destination. Start driving immediately and whenever you face a red light on the road of life, stop and understand that the red light has been put up for your own safety. Once you have understood why you were made to stop, you can then move on with more confidence to reach your destination, wiser than when you started.

Remember, the person who is listless and lazy, lacking the spirit of adventure, is not the one who will achieve great things.

Know in your heart that you have never failed at anything and you never will. But if you insist on using the word 'failure' then just note what one philosopher said –

*'I would rather try to succeed and fail than try to do nothing and succeed.'*

Just know what you want, plan well how to get it and persevere till you succeed…and keep reminding yourself that you cannot fail. *You can only produce results!*

## ELEMENTS OF A FAILURE MECHANISM

F – *Frustration*
A – *Aggressiveness*
I  – *Insecurity*
L – *Loneliness*
U – *Uncertainty*
R – *Resentment*
E – *Emptiness*

—*Dr Maxwell Maltz*

## Something soulful

### WHEN IT LOOKS LIKE I HAVE FAILED...

Lord, are you trying to tell me something? For...

Failure does not mean I am a failure...
It does mean I have yet to succeed.

Failure does not mean I have accomplished nothing...
It does mean I have learned something.

Failure does not mean I have been a fool...
It does mean I had enough faith to experiment.

Failure does not mean I have been disgraced...
It does mean I dared to try.

Failure does not mean I won't have it...
It does mean I have to do something in a different way.

Failure does not mean I am inferior...
It does mean I need to be perfect.

Failure does not mean I have wasted my time...
It does mean I have a reason to start over.

Failure does not mean I should give up...
It does mean I have to try harder.

Failure does not mean I'll never make it...
It does mean I need more patience.

Failure does not mean you have abandoned me...
It does mean you must have a better idea!

*—Author Unknown*

## LIFE IS A JUST EMPLOYER

I bargained with life for a penny, and Life would pay no more,
However I begged at evening, when I counted my scanty store.
For Life is a just employer, he gives you what you ask,
But once you have set the wages, why, you must bear the task.
I worked for a menial's hire, only to learn, dismayed,
That any wage I had asked of Life, Life would have willingly paid.

*—Author Unknown*

## Action plan

1) Actually begin thinking of every failure as a success.

> Every time you fail at something, *you have really succeeded at finding out what does not work.* Therefore, now you are closer to succeeding the next time you try. Refuse to ever use the term 'failure' again about yourself or any one else. Remind yourself that when things don't go as planned, you did not fail. You only produced a different result.

2) Prepare for success. Nobody succeeds without preparation.

> Successful people don't just stumble over a pot of gold. *They spend countless hours getting the knowledge and acquiring the skills that will increase the value of their services.* Are you preparing for your success?

*Inventions That Didn't Succeed:*

*The waterproof towel; glow in the dark sunglasses; solar powered flashlights;*
*submarine screen doors; a book on how to read; inflatable dart boards;*
*a dictionary index; powdered water;*
*waterproof tea bags;*
*the helicopter ejector seat.*

**8**

**Stop Comparing**

## Inspiring thoughts

- When you stop comparing what is right here and now with what you wish were, you can begin to enjoy what is.

  —*Cheri Huber*

- Think of what you have rather than what you lack. Of the things you have, select the best and then reflect how eagerly you would have sought them if you did not have them.

  —*Marcus Aurelius*

- I cried because I had no shoes until I saw a man who had no feet.

  —*Author Unknown*

- Learning to love yourself is the greatest love of all.

  —*Author Unknown*

- Live as you will have wished to have lived when you are dying.

  —*Christian Furchtegott Gellert*

- Judge your success by what you had to give up in order to get it.

  —*Author Unknown*

- When you are content to be simply yourself and don't compare or compete, everybody will respect you.

  —*Lao Tzu*

- If you yourself are not interested in who you are, how can you expect others to be interested in you?

  —*Just* Win *Singh*

You drive through a neighbourhood of bigger homes and nicer cars and you imagine the people who live there are happier than you. You see a glittering polished celebrity on a talk show or in a movie and imagine how great it would be to be like him. You keep feeling that incompleteness which makes you hope if only you were as thin as she is, as smart as he is, as comfortable as they are, somehow your life would be better.

If you identify with any of the above mentioned characteristics, you are living in the comparison trap. You are quite surely, feeling 'lesser' than others and you need to put a conscious stop to your habit of comparing.

In reality, comparison is nothing but a judgement you make based on *what you see and not on what you know*. And what you see is only the glossy surface. Research has shown that many financially successful people are lonely which explains the high rate of suicide in the super rich; many powerful people feel very insecure; many successful business people long for the simple life of a stay-at-home parent. You cannot possibly know the true lives of those you judge by comparison. You can only compare based on appearances. And we all know how incorrect appearances can be.

Comparing how we are faring in life based on how others are faring is dangerous because such comparisons breed tremendous insecurity. Yet we habitually go on comparing. This results in us feeling on top of the world one minute and the very next minute after we have made a comparison, we let inferiority complex set in and destroy our peace of mind.

Quit comparing yourself with others. Instead focus on comparing yourself only with your own personal performance in all walks of life. That is the only true comparison you can ever make. All other things such as people, places, situations, events, emotional feelings, etc. are relative – depending on what they are compared with.

Stop comparing or benchmarking yourself with your peers! Value your own contributions and efforts regardless of what others do. This is the only way to lead a fulfilled life and feel that you have really 'lived' and not wasted your life.

For as long as your eyes are focused on the road others are driving on, you are bound to have an accident on the road you are on yourself. So, turn your head back to your own road and lead yourself on to the destiny you desire to choose.

All the best for your *real* discovery!!

> *We must interpret a bad temper*
> *as a sign of inferiority.*
> —Alfred Adler

## STORY-TIME

*A monkey was having a conversation with a tree.*

*'You mean to tell me,' the monkey said to the tree, 'that you actually stay at one place for an entire lifetime and don't move from that spot? I don't understand!'*

*'You mean to tell me,' the tree said to the monkey, 'that you actually go from place to place using your energy to move about all day? I don't understand!'*

Aren't we all like that? Each one comparing himself with another! Comparing one person to another negates each person's uniqueness and is often insulting to every person's individuality because comparison will never lead to self-knowledge of 'who you really are' ...and this is what your soul is hungry to find out.

God never created a standard person and finally concluded – 'This is it. This is the perfect human.' He made every human being individual and unique just as He made every snowflake and every leaf different. But if we were all supposed to be unique, why do we go on comparing? Probably here is the answer.

## WHY DO WE COMPARE?

We usually look at our behaviour in comparison to others *to judge where we stand in life.* Virtually all our upbringing during childhood (at home and at school) used the comparison method. For the purpose of evaluation, whatever everyone else was doing was consistently used as a barometer to determine what we should be doing.

Before we knew it, the habit of comparison became so prevalent a means of assessment for us, that even in our adult life we began to employ it as our assessment chart. Statistics have proved that more than two-thirds of the people on this planet are validating their performance by comparing theirs with others. So we, too, get tempted to interpret that as the right way.

In our efforts to fit in and be accepted by society, we manage to ambush our real selves by looking to see how we compare to others. In fact, pretending to be like someone has become the greatest past time of the human race. Unfortunately, it has also been the major cause of dissatisfaction in human beings. Why? *Because the most difficult thing in the world is to be who you are not.* And because we are forced to be like someone else, we start feeling that our original self is in some way lesser. And that's what kills our respect for the person we were born to be.

That leads to self-doubt, which causes us to become critical about ourselves and our performance in life. No matter how much we achieve in how many fields, we are still not up to 'their' mark. So we develop a dangerous thing called *an inferiority complex.*

## HOW TO CURE YOUR INFERIORITY COMPLEX?

At least 95% of the people have their lives blighted by feelings of inferiority to some extent and this feeling of inferiority is a serious handicap to their success and happiness.

When you are over critical of yourself, you unknowingly tend to resent people who are doing better. If you have a poor self-image, you will get critical when others do well. You will criticize because you somehow feel inadequate. But on close observation, *you will notice that your criticism has nothing to do with the person you are criticizing. It has to do with your own self-concept.* In fact, your whole happiness depends on how you feel about you.

Your poor self-image which creates this inferiority complex in you needs to be improved. In order to do that you have to simply become aware that you are a unique individual and you don't have to be a carbon copy of your father or brother or neighbour or anybody else. The day you decide to accept this fact, from that day you will start loving the 'self' that God created you as.

If anybody comes shouting at you saying – 'Why can't you be more like your brother?' calmly reply back – 'Because I'm NOT my brother. If I were, I'd be exactly like him, isn't it?' This way, you will keep reminding yourself and others that you were made unique for a reason.

Our culture keeps giving us powerful messages with a model based on power, money, fame, physical appearance or social status. However, it is time we learn to construct a new individualized model based only on what is true for us.

Each one of us is equipped with all the qualities necessary to live our unique life, but it is our job to develop these qualities. From today, *strive for goals that are important to you, not as status symbol, but because they are consistent with your own deep inner wants.* When you strive for 'your' real success, it brings a deep inner satisfaction. Striving for a phony success to please others brings nothing but phony, hollow satisfaction.

Start believing so much in yourself that you don't need the love and approval of other to give you value. If you can just understand and appreciate that there is no common way of living a perfect life, then you will be freer to accept and say – 'This is my way, what is your way?' You will realize that *the* way does not exist.

## COMPARISON IS A TRAP

No matter how hard you try, *there will always be some people who will be more talented, richer, smarter, popular, or wittier than you are.* If you keep playing the comparison game, you will run into too many 'opponents' you can't defeat. And that will cause you great unhappiness.

So simply stop comparing and start living your own unique life. Take your eyes off others. Comparing yourself to anyone is founded in error, inaccurate at best and at worst, brings you the negative energy of judgement and criticism. STOP DOING THAT.

Remember, comparison always puts the controls of your life in the hands of those to whom you compare yourself. Why should you show so much disrespect to the real you that God created and wanted you to be?

Once you cease the habit of continually comparing yourself, you will free yourself to start appreciating others because you will then scrap the destructive notion of – 'If he is more, I am less.' This habit of appreciation will free you to be more loving. *The more love you spread, the more you will be responded with love.* Soon, you will be living the dream life you never thought could become a reality.

The next time you are feeling down as compared to somebody, remind yourself that you are unique in your own way. Affirm to yourself – 'I may not be perfect but I am doing the best I can with the knowledge that I have. I am working at being a better person and I accept myself for the moment.' Then go ahead and work hard on improving yourself to become that better person in your own *eyes and not in the eyes of the world.*

*Wake up to the fact that you are neither inferior nor superior…you are simply YOU…and then go ahead and rejoice in your own individuality.*

## THE PLUM

*You can learn that you cannot be loved by all people.*
*You can be the finest PLUM in the world: ripe, juicy, succulent,*
*And offer yourself to all.*
*However, remember there will always be people who do not like plums.*
*You can learn to understand that if you are the world's best plum*
*And someone you like does not like plums,*
*You have a choice of becoming a banana.*
*However, you need to be warned that if you choose to become a banana,*
*You will be a second-rate banana.*
*However, you can always be the best plum.*
*You need to understand that if you choose to be a second-rate banana,*
*There will always be people who do not like bananas.*
*Furthermore, you can spend your life trying to become the best banana*
*(Which is impossible if you are a plum)*
*Or, you can seek again to be the*
*Best plum in the world.*

—*Author Unknown*

Something soulful

## YOU ARE WORTH IT

Do not undermine your worth by comparing yourself with others.
It is because we are different that each of us is special.
Do not set your goals by what other people deem important.
Only you know what is best for you.
Do not take for granted the things closest to your heart.
Cling to them as you would your life,
For without them, life is meaningless.
Do not let your life slip through your fingers
By living in the past nor for the future.
By living your life one day at a time,
you live all the days of your life.
Do not give up when you still have something to give.
Nothing is really over until the moment you stop trying.
It is a fragile thread that binds us to each other.
Do not be afraid to encounter risks.
It is by taking chances that we learn how to be brave.
Do not shut love out of your life by saying it is impossible to find.
The quickest way to receive love is to give love;
The fastest way to lose love is to hold it too tightly.
Do not dismiss your dreams.
To be without dreams is to be without hope;
To be without hope is to be without purpose.
Do not run through life so fast that you forget
Not only where you have been, but also where you are going.
Life is not a race, but a journey
To be savoured each step of the way.

—*Author Unknown*

## THE MOUNTAIN & THE SQUIRREL

The mountain and the squirrel, had a quarrel;
And the former called the latter 'Little Prig.'
Bun replied, 'Doubtless you are very big;
But all sorts of things and weather must be taken in together
To make up a year and a sphere.
And I think it's no disgrace to occupy my place.
If I'm not so large as you, you are not so small as I.
And not half so spry.
I'll not deny you make, a very pretty squirrel track;
Talents differ: all is well and wisely put;
If I cannot carry forests on my back,
Neither can you crack a nut.'

—*Ralph Waldo Emerson*

## Action plan

1) Make a transition from comparing yourself to improving yourself. From now onwards, start evaluating yourself and your performances on your own personal index.

> *Start measuring your growth this year in terms of your own progress last year, rather than against the progress of your neighbour.* This is the only way you will ever be able to draw your level of satisfaction.

2) Stop comparing yourself with others by admiring their gifts and ignoring your own gifts.

> Most people dwell on their inadequacies and then wonder why their life is not working out. The next time you feel inferior, pinch yourself and then immediately *start focusing on your positive traits* (are you honest? helpful? loving?) and you will surely start liking yourself again and this is the doorway to enjoy life.

> *At a party a young man approached a beautiful woman and asked: 'What sort of a man are you looking for to get married?' The woman replied: 'Well, he should be intelligent like Albert Einstein, charming like Clark Gable, rugged like Clint Eastwood, good-looking like Tom Cruise and witty and funny like Woody Allen.' The boy instantly replied: 'How fortunate we met.'*

**9**

**Jaundice of Jealousy**

## Inspiring thoughts

- Jealousy is the jaundice of the soul.

  —*John Dryden*

- I would rather be able to appreciate things I cannot have than to have things I am not able to appreciate.

  —*Author Unknown*

- Jealousy is all the fun you think *they* had.

  —*Erica Jong*

- Measure your wealth by what you'd have left if you lost all your money.

  —*Author Unknown*

- It is not love that produces jealousy; it is selfishness.

  —*Justice Wallington*

- Love looks through a telescope; jealousy through a microscope.

  —*Josh Billings*

- Jealousy is a tribute that the weak pay to the strong.

  —*Author Unknown*

- Jealousy is a mental cancer.

  —*B C Forbes*

- To cure jealousy is to see it for what it is – a dissatisfaction with self.

  —*Joan Didion*

- Jealousy is the knife of your own insecurities with which you stab others.

  —*Just* Win *Singh*

The subject of comparisons is such a strong cause of unhappiness in human beings that we are forced to dedicate another chapter on it. In this chapter we will take up the deeper emotion called *Jealousy – which is caused by magnifying our habit of comparing.*

Every emotion has been given to us for a reason. Our envious nature, thus, also serves a purpose. Small doses of envy can help motivate us. When someone else has what we want, our envious nature can increase our determination to get it.

Unfortunately, over the years, the emotion of envy has slowly been poisoned by that of jealousy. Before we get to the core of the subject, it becomes important for us to understand the clear-cut distinction between envy (which is a natural emotion) and jealousy (which is a learned emotion). Envy is the emotion that makes a toddler wish he could reach a door knob the way his brother can, or ride a bike. Envy is a natural emotion that makes us want to do it again, to try harder and to continue striving until we succeed. It is, in fact, healthy to be envious.

However, our society has enforced on children to believe that envy is not okay, that it is wrong to express it. So, they continually repress this natural emotion. *Envy that is continuously repressed becomes jealousy,* which is the unnatural and harmful emotion that has even made people kill others. While envy motivates us to improve ourselves and get what we want, jealousy makes us wish that nobody gets anything better than us. For a jealous person, it becomes second nature that *instead of deriving pleasure from what he has, he derives pain from what others have.*

Jealousy almost always originates in our feelings of inadequacy. We feel we are inadequate to have or be what we think we see others having or being. In today's competitive world, it's not unusual to desire what someone else has but if we let those emotions get the best of us, we could do ourselves more harm than good.

Feeling jealous stems from a fundamental error in thinking. Adults and children alike tend to think that we can and should always get what we want. And if we can't and someone else can, we scream – 'It's just not fair!'

If you are the comparing type, it is essential you carefully study this chapter. And after going through this chapter, if you immediately started comparing it with the previous one, then you just caught yourself doing the very thing which was suggested you not to do.

Beware! You HAVE TO break out of this web of comparisons if you really want to live the life you were made for. Don't look outside…look inside and search the true meaning of life for you.

> *A competent and self-confident person is incapable of jealousy in anything. Jealousy is invariably a symptom of neurotic insecurity.*
> —Robert A. Heinlein

You have been blessed with a beautiful car but the moment your neighbour drives a so-called latest brand, you automatically start feeling like a third class child of God. Suddenly, you start noticing all the defects in your own car.

You go for a movie and out of the blues you clash into your handsome colleague whom your wife adores, and in an instant you wish you had never come there at all. Why? Because you are caught in the pangs of jealousy!

Every human being, at some time or another, gets caught up with the emotion of jealousy that transforms him into a green-eyed monster which not only consumes those around him, but also consumes him from the inside.

Feelings of jealousy always appear to stem from one's sense that something about their lives is insecure. The word 'jealousy' comes from the Greek word 'jeal.' It suggests that a valued possession is in danger and that some action must be taken. *Jealousy, therefore, is usually a signal of something needing fixing and ignoring that usually makes things worse.*

Jealousy has no limits and can run into every area of our lives, but we shall take up the two basic areas where almost everyone can identify with jealous behaviour – firstly, jealousy of material wealth, and secondly, jealousy in relationships. Let's study these two vital areas a little further.

## COMPETITION CREATES MATERIALISTIC JEALOUSY

Unfortunately, our whole education system is rooted in jealousy. We point to one child and say to the other, 'See how intelligent he is and how dull you are. Be like him!' Thus, we create jealousy and hatred from our childhood days.

Slowly, the human heart, as modern civilization has made it, has become more prone to hatred than to friendship. And it is prone to hatred because it is dissatisfied. And it is dissatisfied because everybody is being told to be up to the mark like somebody else. So while one tries to be like another, the other is trying to be like a third person and the vicious cycle never ends. Ultimately, everybody is unhappy.

*The entire trouble starts from the general philosophy of life where we are preaching life as a contest, a competition, in which respect will be accorded only to the victor.* The whole educational system is based on the fever of getting ahead of everyone else, and this fever persists even after the children come out of the field of education. They now want bigger homes, bigger cars, higher positions, etc.

To add fuel to fire, the amount of money made by someone, has become the accepted measure of how brainy he is. So everybody strives to outdo the other. What do they achieve in the end? *Wherever they reach, they find someone ahead of them. As long as there is someone ahead, there is no peace.* Then the race goes on and on. The irony is that most of them will remain in that race throughout their lives and will, in the process, literally miss out on life itself.

## STOP COMPETING & START ADMIRING

We must realize that too much emphasis on competition kills the very hope of love between fellow humans and flames the uncontrolled sparks of hatred. *We need to change our focus immediately.*

We all know that each soul has a mission, the very reason for anyone being born on this Earth. Nature equips each of us with whatever we need to fulfill our special purpose. If we don't know what our mission is, the very things we have or don't have may provide us with some clues.

For instance, musical talents point us in one direction while intellectual gifts point us in another. Poverty may push us to accomplish something in the business world while compassion may drive us to help others. The gifts and talents we possess are the very tools we need to fulfill our purpose. Consequently, once you understand this basic fact, what your neighbour has *becomes completely irrelevant.* You will realize that there is absolutely no point in comparing since it has nothing to do with your purpose.

As they say, the baker isn't envious of the tailor's scissors. Likewise, it is senseless to lust after someone's wealth, since it can't help to do what we were sent here to do.

The best way to transform your outlook of jealousy of material wealth is to develop a compensating passion, namely that of ADMIRATION. Whoever wishes to increase human happiness must wish to increase admiration and diminish jealousy as beautifully stated in the story below.

## STORY-TIME

*A millionaire who had ostentatiously displayed a blaze of his diamonds was heartily thanked by a person in the crowd. 'What do you mean?' he asked, 'I never gave you any of my diamonds. Then why are you thanking me?'*

*To this the stranger replied, 'No, you never gave me any of the diamonds. But you have let me look at them and that is all the use you can make of them yourself. So there is no difference between us, except that you have the trouble of watching them and that is an employment I do not desire.'*

Moral of the story: Why should we not feel rich in all that our eyes can carry away, no matter if others happen to have the title deed? If you are not wealthy yourself, be glad that somebody else is and you will be astonished at the happiness you will feel yourself. Simple! Try it.

## JEALOUSY IN RELATIONSHIPS

We all know that feeling a strong emotion is necessary to make changes. In this way, feelings of jealousy in a relationship are not always bad because through such feelings we acquire the insight which causes us to appreciate the value of another person. These jealous feelings can bring our neurotic needs to the surface and thus cause us to change our behaviour.

Loyalty in a relationship is based upon trust and respect. *Jealousy takes root when this trust is demanded instead of being offered.* When you demand loyalty, you never get it. The only way to get loyalty and trust is to offer it, never demand it. Get this clear.

Once we can feel the pangs of jealousy in a relationship, we must understand that jealousy is most often a product of our personal insecurity and low esteem. It occurs because we see ourselves as having less to give than the object of our jealousy.

Don't be afraid to feel jealous. You may not be able to control that. However, the important decision will be whether you will allow jealousy to become an all-consuming monster, capable of destroying you and those you love, or will you take it as a challenge to charge yourself up to grow in self-respect and personal knowledge. This challenge will entirely rest on you.

It is time we finally accept the fact that *we can never possess another human being*. We must learn that loving others is not about possessing them but letting them be themselves, painful as it may be, with or without you.

Let us no more feel jealous for the jealous man lives in his self-created Hell. Accept the fact that the idea of 'the other' enters our head because we have not allowed our own blissfulness to grow. Hence, we feel empty and tend to start comparing. And in our comparisons, if we have a low self-esteem, we often fall short of others. That gives rise to jealousy.

From today, drop your habit of comparing and jealousy will disappear. And to drop your habit of comparing, you will have to start growing your inner treasures. *There is no other way to grow beyond this emotion.*

## SHIFT YOUR FOCUS

*Try to shift your focus from what others have or don't have to what you are going to do for yourself.*

*Have an inner belief that anyone who has achieved prosperity is entitled to it and his success is no reason for you to feel inadequate or wanting.*

*Even if you feel a person has achieved prosperity through what you consider devious means, it is still no reason for you to feel upset.*

*Know in your heart that any wrongs by others will be dealt with by a Universe that works on purpose and harmony.*

—Dr Wayne Dyer

Something soulful

## ANYWAY

People are often unreasonable, illogical, and self-centred;
*Forgive them anyway.*

If you are kind, people may accuse you of selfish, ulterior motives;
*Be kind anyway.*

If you are successful, you will win some false friends and
some true enemies;
*Succeed anyway.*

If you are honest and frank, people may cheat you;
*Be honest and frank anyway.*

What you spend years building, someone could destroy overnight;
*Build anyway.*

If you find serenity and happiness, they may be jealous;
*Be happy anyway.*

The good you do today, people will often forget tomorrow;
*Do good anyway.*

Give the world the best you have, and it may never be enough.
*Give the world the best you've got anyway.*

You see, in the final analysis, it is between you and God;
*It was never between you and them anyway.*

—*Author Unknown*

## BE THE BEST OF WHATEVER YOU ARE

If you can't be a highway,
Then just be a trail.
If you can't be the sun,
Be a star.
It isn't by the size
That you win or fail –
Be the best of whatever you are!

—*Douglas Mallach*

## Action plan

1) Instead of focusing on others, focus on yourself. Sit down in a quiet place and seriously give it a thought – What is it that inspires you in life? If you are sincere in your effort, you will surely get your answer.

> *Whatever inspires you deep down your heart is your real purpose of life.* Once you have identified that, all you need to do is take steps to achieve it. (Clue: your true purpose in life will be something that gets you really excited and you can't have enough of it; something that gets you so involved that you forget everything else and live in that very moment without even bothering about any food or water.)

2) When you feel jealous in your relationship, ask yourself – 'What do I feel insecure about?'

> Identify why you feel 'lesser' compared to the person who is your object of jealousy. Where do you feel you may be lacking? Is it that you are not as caring as you should be? Is it that you have taken someone for granted? *Find out the lack that makes you lesser* and then simply work to outshine the other person.

*My wife's jealousy is getting ridiculous. The other day she looked at my calendar and wanted to know who was – 'MAY.'*

# 10

## Stop Wishing and
## Start Fishing

## Inspiring thoughts

- He that is good at making excuses is seldom good for anything else

  —*Benjamin Franklin*

- Many of us spend half our time wishing for things we could have if we didn't spend half our time wishing.

  —*Alexander Woollcott*

- Ninety nine percent of the failures come from people who have the habit of making excuses.

  —*G. W. Carver*

- Excuses are the nails used to build a house of failure.

  —*Don Wilder*

- The trick is not how much pain you feel but how much joy you feel. Any idiot can feel pain. Life is full of excuses not to live... excuses, excuses, excuses.

  —*Erica Jong*

- The happiest people don't just *get* the best of everything. They just *make* the best of everything.

  —*Author Unknown*

- My wish isn't to mean everything to everybody but something to someone.

  —*Author Unknown*

- If wishes were horses, beggars would ride.

  —*Proverb*

- A happy life is your main responsibility. So start responding with ability.

  —*Just* Win *Singh*

Have you ever got the feeling that you are wasting your life? Have you felt the snake of discontentment creep onto you to make you feel uneasy in the abdomen? You know why do you feel like that? It is because you might be consciously ignoring your own needs and desires but your subconscious mind does not forget what you want to be and it keeps reminding you constantly through your anger, stress, sadness, insecurity and feelings of failure… *because you are doing something and desiring something else.*

If you want to get out of this ruthless feeling of incompleteness, you must immediately start listening to yourself and become your best friend and supporter you need, because no one is going to work on your happiness for you.

Too many people neglect themselves, feeling that it would be selfish if they took any time to focus on their own being. While it is good to care for others and other important things going on in your life, you must NEVER forget about yourself.

Making *you* first priority is not selfish. It actually is obligatory to do so in order to succeed in all areas of your life. Without a happy and satisfied you, how can you have a happy and satisfied life…and in turn, how can you spread happiness?

If on the other hand you are neglecting your wishes because you do not want to put in the desired effort then you are like the non-achiever who keeps saying – '*I would if I could, but I can't so I won't.*'

This way you can never get what you wish for. And you have the good chance of becoming a complainer in life since you will never be able to succeed in anything and so you will take your revenge by speaking ill of this world.

On the other hand, if you change your attitude to – '*If I try, I might. If I don't, I won't,*' then you are taking full responsibility for your life and happiness. You are then, no more an excuse specialist. And you have all the possibility to make your wishes a reality.

If you claim to have many dreams but keep saying that you don't have the time, the education, the money, the opportunity... then it's time for you to – STOP MAKING EXCUSES! They are nothing but stop signs that halt your progress.

You are the only one who holds the power to make a real difference in your life. And remember, your mission in life is not to be without problems...

...*Your mission in life is to get EXCITED!!!*

> *A goal without a plan is*
> *just a wish.*
> —Larry Elder

## STORY-TIME

*A Persian king summoned the three wisest men in his realm and asked: 'What is the greatest evil of life?'*

*The wise men thought for a while. Then the first man spoke: 'Life's greatest evil is to have debts and not have money to pay.'*

*Then the second man spoke: 'Of all the evils, the greatest is to be sick and not have a cure.'*

*Finally, the third wise man came up with his solution: 'The greatest evil in life,' he said, 'is to stand at the end of it and to know that is was wasted.'*

How many of us simply exist instead of actually living a life we wish to live? How many of us have sleepless nights because we get the feeling that we have wasted another day? In fact, most people are scared of death because they *know* they have not yet started living.

# WHY DO WE MAKE EXCUSES?

Why is it that we hear people wishing for something and not getting it? On close observation, it will become clear that *most people are not ready to put in the required effort to make their dreams a reality.* And so their guilt of not achieving what they could, develops in them an extremely useless habit – that of making excuses.

Excuses negate responsibility and it is responsibility that separates man from the rest of the animal kingdom. Unlike other animals, we are responsible not only for what we have but also for what we could have; not only for what we are, but also for what we could become.

*If you look around, you will observe that the more successful the individual the less inclined he is to make excuses.* Studies of the lives of happily successful people have revealed a very important fact: all the excuses made by the average fellow could be *but aren't* made by the successful people.

Unfortunately most people have arrived at the idea that if they have enough excuses and things to blame, it is alright to be miserable. But remember, you may have a wish list as long as the Great Wall of China, but till you start living the life you want to live, no excuse is any compensation.

Most people have unfulfilled dreams because they are not very honest with themselves. They say things are *impossible* when the truth is they are *very inconvenient.* Also, such people prefer an excuse to an achievement because an achievement leaves them having to prove themselves again in the future *but an excuse can easily last for life.* So they stay in their miserable state convincing themselves as to why go fishing...it's easier to keep wishing.

## STOP THINKING 'IF ONLY...'

If you are the kind who keeps stating 'If only I could get a better break,' 'If only I had the money,' 'If only I would have married the right person,' 'If only my parents had brought me up in a better way,' 'If only...' then it is very essential for you to stop this 'wishing' habit right now.

You may think that a parent, boss, spouse, company or some governmental programme should shoulder your burden for turning your life into what you want it to be. Unfortunately, this approach can never get the job done because other people have their own pressing problems. This means that you will always be disappointed when you depend on others for the things you must do for yourself.

'If only' wishers are the most frustrated people on earth because they have created their own frustrations due to lack of self-faith. And it is very clear that you can never be successful and happy until you earn the respect of the toughest and the most important judge in the world: *yourself*.

If you feel you have fallen into the 'wishing' trap, what you need is a simple *reboot of your passion for life* to get you back on track. You need to 'Control – Alt – Delete' yourself (as you do in your computer).

## USE THE 'CONTROL – ALT – DELETE' TECHNIQUE

CONTROL: Who is in control of your attitude? When you feel stuck, you lose the control, the focus and the passion for achieving your dreams. First and foremost, you must, regain your CONTROL. If your ship of life is in danger, you are the most capable captain to control it.

ALT          : Life is full of ALTERNATIVES. When you are stuck, you have probably made a few wrong choices and now you feel down, frozen and locked up. Begin today to look for alternatives. Stop taking the easy road of being lazy and lying back hopelessly. Stop listening to negative inputs and instead begin to listen to that inner voice that started and ignited your passion or dream in the first place. Stop making excuses for your condition in life. Instead, search for alternatives to make improvements in yourself to make you better.

DELETE     : Erase, remove, cancel, cross out all the negative things that have held you back, be it a habit, an association, or simply your newspaper. Are there people with negative attitudes giving you advice? DELETE them from your ife. These negatives have made you lose your belief in the possibility of happily succeeding. Get rid of them. This is the most difficult action to take, but you must take it for your own happiness.

Once you have Control – Alt – Deleted, you will be back to your original settings (ie. passion, desire, dreams) that started you on the road of your personal success and happiness. Then you can BE, DO & HAVE whatever you wish for.

## FOLLOW THE 'BE-DO-HAVE' PRINCIPLE
## OF HAPPINESS

Often people attempt to live their lives backwards: they try to HAVE more things or more money, in order to DO more of what they want so that they will BE happier. The way it actually works is quite the reverse. You must first BE who you really are, then DO what you need to do in order to HAVE what you really want.

How many times have you looked at others and thought, 'I wish I could be that happy,' 'I wish I could be that confident,'? Though it's not unhealthy to see, in other people, qualities and characteristics that you would like to emulate, but the essential issue for you is to understand why you haven't been able to be the way you wish to be.

As a child you may not have had the power or knowledge to make your own choices, but now, as an adult who is stopping you?

## BE REALISTIC IN WHAT YOU WISH FOR

*The biggest mistake that people make is aiming too high too soon.* Say, if you plan to be a tennis champ, it would be a good idea to first learn how to hold the racket and hit the ball across the net.

Honestly, if it is to be, it is up to you. If you want your life to get better, you must get better. If you want things to improve, you must first improve yourself. Following your dream is no guarantee for an easy ride. *Doing what you love is not a recipe for an easier life. It is simply a recipe for an interesting life.*

Discover who you really are and what matters to you. Living a great life does not just happen. It requires planning your priorities and making effort for achieving them. The only way to live a happy and satisfied life is when you start doing things that make you happy and satisfied.

Remember you have but one life to live. If you go to the grave with a list of 'reasons why I didn't,' all it means is that you kept wishing but never went fishing.

## PLANT YOUR GARDEN OF SUCCESS TODAY

*First, plant 3 rows of Peas*    *– Patience,    Positive    thinking, Persistence.*

*Next, plant 3 rows of Squash*    *– Squash  excuses,  Squash  blame, Squash criticism.*

*Then, plant 3 rows of Lettuce*    *– Let  us  be  responsible,  Let  us  be trustworthy, Let us be ambitious.*

*Finish, with 3 rows of Turnip*    *– Turn up when needed, Turn up with a smile, Turn up with confidence.*

—Chuck Gallozzi

*Something soulful*

# EQUIPMENT

Figure it out for yourself, my lad,
You've all that the greatest of men have had,
Two arms, two hands, two legs, two eyes,
And a brain to use if you would be wise.
With this equipment they all began,
Do start from the top and say, 'I can!'

Look them over, the wise and the great,
They take their food from a common plate,
And similar knives and forks they use,
With similar laces they tie their shoes.
The world considers them brave and smart,
But you've all they had, when they made their start.

You can triumph and come to skill,
You can be great if you only will.
You're well equipped for what fight you choose,
You have arms and legs and a brain to use...
And the man who has risen great deeds to do,
Began his life with no more than you.

You are the handicap you must face,
You are the one, who must choose his place,
You must say where you want to go,
How much you will study, the truth to know.
God has equipped you for life, but He
Lets you decide what you want to be.

Courage must come from the soul within,
The man must furnish the will to win.
So figure it out for yourself, my lad,
You were born with all the great have had.
With your equipment they all began,
Get hold of yourself, and say, 'I can!'

—*Edgar Guest*

## IT'S WHAT YOU DO DO

It's not what you *can* do,
It's not what you *will* do,
It's what you *do* do.

—*Author Unknown*

## Action plan

1) Eliminate the words 'hope,' 'wish,' and 'maybe,' from your vocabulary. They are the tools for postponing your happiness.

> Change – 'I hope things will work out' to 'I will make it happen.' Change – 'I wish things will be better' to 'I am going to do so & so to ensure that things will be better.' Don't just sit back and hope. *Be a doer rather than a wisher.*

2) If you were relieved of all practical considerations (say you won millions of dollars and no more needed the money) – what would be the first thing that you would do?

> Take your time to answer this question because it helps to make your fantasies conscious. This is the ideal way for you to be focused to *work towards what makes you happy and not on what others term as happiness for you.* Remember, no two answers to happiness are alike because no two people are alike.

*'It's not easy to get ahead in this world,' a businessman assured a young friend. 'As a lad I started out at the bottom. I struggled, worked, sweated, climbing the ladder of life hand over hand, rung by rung.' 'And now,' interposed the lad, 'you are a great success?' 'Well, no,' admitted the businessman, 'but I'm getting mighty good at climbing ladders.'*

# 11

## What is Luck?

## Inspiring thoughts

- Destiny is not a matter of chance, it is a matter of choice; it is not a thing to be waited for, it is a thing to be achieved.

  —*William Jennings Bryan*

- You don't get paid for the hour. You get paid for the *value* you bring to the hour.

  —*Jim Rohn*

- The harder I practice, the luckier I get.

  —*Gary Player*

- When the going gets tough, the tough get going.

  —*Author Unknown*

- Big shots are the little shots that keep shooting.

  —*Christopher Morley*

- Luck is the tide, nothing more. The strong man rows with it if it makes toward his port; he rows against it if it flows the other way.

  —*Author Unknown*

- Genius is 1% inspiration and 99% perspiration.

  —*Thomas Edison*

- What counts is not necessarily the size of the dog in the fight; it's the fight in the dog.

  —*Dwight Eisenhower*

- Good luck is a residue of preparation.

  —*Jack Youngblood*

- How to make your luck? Just be prepared when opportunity knocks.

  —*Just* Win *Singh*

The Chinese call 'luck' opportunity and they say that opportunity knocks every day at your door. Some people hear it and some people don't.

Those who hear it are already making their own luck. However, many don't hear the knocks (or don't want to because they are lazy) and they are *ironically happy in blaming* their luck for their distressful state in life.

Studies have shown that although wealth can be inherited, individual success cannot be. It is neither genetic nor environmental. Otherwise, why is it that when two identical twins are raised in the same environment, one can grow to be a successful businessman while the other becomes a homeless alcoholic?

The answer lies in the CHOICES each of those individuals made at various stages in their lives…even though *initially* life offered them exactly the same chance.

There is no word in the English language more misused and abused than 'luck.' More people have excused themselves for their poor work and performance by saying 'luck was against them' than by any other plea. Such people do not realize that praying for a miracle will rarely make their dreams come true.

*Depending on luck is like walking with crutches.* But remember, crutches are intended for cripples and not able bodied people like you and me and if you intend to go through life on mental crutches (of bad luck) you will not go far and will never know what it is to be happily successful.

On close scrutiny you will observe that the 'lucky' man is a logical thinker, a finer judge, more systematic and disciplined and much more practical that the 'unlucky' man. He does whatever it takes to achieve whatever he desires. He does not keep dreaming but is actually doing what is necessary to get what he wants. And he does not bother to wait for an auspicious occasion on some later date.

He knows that the dream of doing something someday can come true only when he changes *someday* to *today*. Someday is NOW.

Remember, luck is nothing but a re-configuration of events and on the path of your happiness and success, nobody can ever stop you but yourself.

So go and **L**abour **U**nder **C**orrect **K**nowledge...and LUCK will be yours.

> *The only time 'success' comes before*
> *'work' is in the dictionary.*
> —Vidal Sassoon

## EXPERIMENT TIME

*Suppose we were to show you a gambling game in which you NEVER LOSE, would you be interested? Well, take out a coin. The play consists of tossing the coin to see how it lands. Obviously, it can only fall either Heads or Tails. Let's say, you pick Heads. Let Heads stand for whatever you want in life – more money, more happiness, a better job, you name it.*

*Now toss the coin...It landed Heads? Congratulations, you have won whatever you wanted on the very first try.*

*But suppose it didn't land Heads up and say it landed Tails up instead. No problem. Don't get disheartened because here's the wonderful thing about this game: Even though the coin didn't land the way you wanted, that doesn't diminish your chances of success. Why? Because in this game (as in the game of life) there is no penalty when the coin doesn't land right. You can keep on tossing, again and again, as often as you like, until it does land right.*

*In other words, YOU CANNOT LOSE…if you keep tossing the coin. Moral of the story: If you keep trying, you will finally always WIN.*

That's exactly how the game of success and happiness is played in real life. If you *keep trying*, you are a certain winner.

We can easily conclude from the above game, that nobody is ever unlucky. Good luck follows sheer hard work and if you keep persisting, no bad luck can stop you.

## DEFINITION OF LUCK

*Luck is defined as a force that brings good fortune or adversity; the events or circumstances that operate for or against an individual.*

Since it is a force, it can surely be used to your advantage. Unfortunately, most people never realize that good fortune is *caused*. Wanting something intensely is the motivating power that produces good luck.

You don't agree? Well, give it a thought – what has *chance* ever done in this world? Has it invented the telephone? Has it made the light bulb? Has it built all the bridges, tunnels, hospitals, universities, automobiles, space crafts?

Still not convinced! Well, let's study the 3 kinds of Luck in more detail to understand better.

## THREE KINDS OF LUCK

If you study more deeply, you will come across three kinds of luck:

**Luck by Accident:** This kind of luck is unplanned and you have little or no control over it. Natural disasters, physical handicaps, etc. fit this category. Life just happens to you. Your company goes bankrupt and you get laid off. Your car gets stolen. *You cannot influence such luck but you can only respond to it.* You can only learn from the experience and do nothing more.

**Luck by Opportunity:** Here you need to see the opportunity and be prepared to take advantage of it. A timely response is essential in this case. The seat next to the girl you admire so dearly is empty. Here is an opportunity for you to sit next to her and get acquainted and take it from there. *You must be prepared to take advantage of this opportunity.* (As they say – 'Chance favours the prepared mind.')

**Luck by Design:** Say you are looking for a job. You read every possible newspaper and magazine looking for leads. You browse the internet sites. You talk to everyone you know. You tell whosoever will listen what you are looking for. And finally, you get the job you want. This is what luck by design is. *You know what you want and you simply work to get lucky.* In other words, we can term it as *planned luck.*

Take the case of President Lincoln:
1831 – Failed in business
1832 – Defeated for a seat in the Legislature
1833 – Again failed in business
1834 – Elected to the Legislature
1835 – Sweetheart died
1836 – Had a nervous breakdown
1838 – Defeated for Speaker
1840 – Defeated for Elector
1843 – Defeated for Land Officer
1843 – Defeated for Congress
1846 – Elected to Congress
1848 – Defeated for Congress
1855 – Defeated for Senate
1856 – Lost nomination for Vice-President
1858 – Defeated for Senate
1860 – Elected President

Would you call him lucky to become the President? Before he became the President, he was unlucky a number of times. But instead of blaming luck, he studied his setbacks as a part of his political education. *He resolved to take fate by the throat and shake a living out of her.* And today he is known as one of the sharpest, most unbeatable human beings that ever lived. He is an ideal example of Luck by Design.

It is important to remember that while you cannot control Luck by Accident, you can surely influence both Luck by Opportunity and Luck by Design. In short, if you wish, you can definitely increase your chances of being lucky. To feel fulfilled and happy at any stage of your life, you must (if you already haven't) learn to make your own luck.

Since luck is nothing but the *intersection of preparation & opportunity* and since opportunity is always available, the individuals who are especially prepared always seem to win while the unprepared ones rationalize their failure as a 'run of bad luck.'

## HOW TO MAKE YOUR OWN LUCK?

*When you believe in luck and sit back fretting, you are slapping yourself in the face. You are insulting your own ability to take disciplined action.* You are disparaging your own capacity to achieve the results you desire. And you become a victim of life.

But if you are a believer in luck, then the bitter truth is that you are not ready to make a thorough preparation for success. You are not ready to pay the price for it and are instead, looking for bargains and hunting for short cuts to your happiness.

Even if you get lucky and obtain something for nothing, it would be mostly worthless because the value you seek cannot truly be yours without the discipline, effort, action and persistence necessary to create that value.

Don't try to justify your failure on the ground that you have been doomed by the cards that fate has dealt you. You have the power within you to *change the value* of the cards. Don't wait for some outside power to lift you into a position of comfort and luxury in some mysterious way so that very little effort is needed from your end.

Life is not a game of chance. Good luck follows good sense, good intention, good judgement, good health, a strong determination, a lofty ambition and sheer hard work. The day you use your good sense in applied hard work *without ever giving up,* that's when good luck will start happening to you.

Don't join the gang of people who believe in 'tough luck,' 'hard luck,' 'bad luck,' for these people are still little children, immature and searching for sympathy. Instead of wasting your mental muscles dreaming of an effortless way to win success, commit yourself to hard work towards whatever you want to achieve. Your commitment to hard work will create such a force field of positive energy around you that it will attract other positive people and greater opportunities into your life.

*Stop using your wishbone and start using your backbone...and see your luck change.*

## MEN CALLED IT LUCK

*He worked by day, and toiled by night*
*He gave up play, and some delight.*
*Dry books he read, new things to learn*
*And forged ahead, success to earn.*
*He plodded on with, faith and pluck*
*And when he won, men called it LUCK.*

—*Anonymous*

Something soulful

## MAKE YOUR OWN LUCK

When your belief in yourself you chuck,
That's when you start believing in luck.

When you can't solve your problems and feel stuck,
That's when you start believing in luck.

When you are lazy and float around like a duck,
That's when you start believing in luck.

When you fail to earn a really fast buck,
That's when you start believing in luck.

Wake up and strive for goals of good cause
And you'll never again say – 'It was because…'

Work hard for the things you desire,
And see how your luck catches fire.

Get up and work towards your goal,
And luck will support you from the soul.

Help others in their dreams to succeed
And luck will join you in your good deed.

Face the mirror and deeply look there
Are you going to get it or just going to stare?

Life goes on and people do make it
Go make your own luck, don't forsake it.

—*Just* Win *Singh*

## WHAT HELPS LUCK

What helps luck is a habit of watching for opportunities,
Of having a patient but restless mind,
Of sacrificing one's ease and vanity,
Of uniting a love of detail to foresight,
And of passing through hard times bravely and cheerfully.

—*Victor Cherbuliez*

## Action plan

1) When you see someone doing better than you under similar circumstances, don't think he is more luckier. Instead try and find out why you are lagging behind.

> Just say to yourself – *'There must be some reason for his success.* There must be a secret 'something' at the back of it that I may not be doing, and I am going to find out what it is.' This is better than pleading hard luck for yourself and good fortune for another.

2) Make a resolution that no matter what happens, you will never give up. Remember the coin experiment we did where everybody wins at one stage or another.

> When you back up your goals with unshakable determination and persistence, you will eventually find that *there is nothing in the world that can stop a man who never gives up.*

'He has always been lucky in love.'
'You mean he always gets his women?'
'No – he's still a bachelor.'

# 12

**Be a No-Limits Person**

## Inspiring thoughts

- The truest definition I know of a no-limit person is simply a person who knows how to enjoy life, especially when those around him are getting mad.

  —*Dr Wayne Dyer*

- The average man does not want to be *free*. He simply wants to be *safe*.

  —*H. L. Mencken*

- Needing approval is tantamount to saying – 'Your view of me is more important than my own opinion of myself.'

  —*Author Unknown*

- Care about people's approval and you will be their prisoners.

  —*Tao Te Ching*

- Growth is impossible if a person always does things the way everyone has always done things.

  —*Author Unknown*

- A man who limits his interests, limits his life.

  —*Vincent Price*

- While you are wishing to be someone else, someone, somewhere is wishing to be you.

  —*Author Unknown*

- A man cannot be comfortable without his own approval.

  —*Mark Twain*

- Authentic freedom is when you can be who you are wherever you are.

  —*Just* Win *Singh*

From his birth a child is told what is right, what is wrong. He is never given the freedom to choose on his own and he grows up following a set of principles which his elders insist are correct for him. Whenever he does anything on his own, he is disapproved (and often punished) by his family, society, school, and practically everybody.

So, the child loses his confidence and becomes shaky. He then gets conditioned to *take approval* just to do about anything. This develops his approval-seeking attitude. Even though his body grows, his mind remains chained to the habit of approval seeking.

Haven't we all been following so many meaningless rules set by society in the name of etiquette or good manners? Think of all the little foolish rules you have been encouraged to adopt simply because some individual (Emily Post, Vanderbilt, or even your eldest relative alive) has asked you to do so in the name of correct behaviour.

If you have ever behaved in a certain way because you *should* have done do so (and not because you *wanted* to) you would quite certainly have experienced a feeling of strain. Now, since every step of your life has been designed to follow a set of rules (sometimes laid generations ago) you are constantly under a subconscious strain.

If you have to take every breath of your life under the surveillance of a certain rule, always strained by shoulds, should nots, musts, must nots, this is right, that is wrong, soften your voice, don't laugh, its time to sleep, its time to get up...how can you even breathe freely, leave alone be happy?

That's why you feel frustrated since you want to do something in your own unique way but you are being guided by society to do something else just because *that's the way it has always been done.*

It's time to stop evaluating yourself on the basis of what someone else feels or felt. Break away from certain rules which you may be blindly following and which may be limiting your experience of happiness.

But beware! You must not rebel just for the sake of rebelling. You need not go about highlighting your rule-breaking behaviour since your aim here is to simply break free from *useless* rules and not to win attention (otherwise you are back on the other side of the same approval seeking posture).

It is tougher to handle rebuke and easier to adopt behaviour that brings approval, but by taking this easier path, *you are making others' opinion of you more important than your own self-assessment.* And as long as your happiness depends on what others think of you, your happiness is in someone else's hands.

You can decide to be the person you want to be, or the one that others want you to be. The choice is entirely up to you! Here's a chance to choose your own freedom.

> *A truly strong person does not need the approval of others any more than a lion needs the approval of sheep.*
> —Vernon Howard

## STORY-TIME

*A wife sent her husband to the store to buy some ham. After he bought it, she asked him why he didn't have the butcher cut off the end of the ham. The man asked his wife why she always wanted the end cut off. She replied that her mother had always done it that way and that was reason enough for her.*

*Since the wife's mother was visiting, they asked her why she always cut off the end of the ham. Mother replied that this was the way her mother did it. Mother, daughter and the man then decided to call grandmother to solve this three generation mystery.*

*Grandmother promptly replied that she cut the end of the ham off because her roaster was too small to cook it in one piece. Now grandma had a reason for her actions. But what about her daughter and her grand daughter? They were blindly following (without question) the method of cooking for no reason other than, 'It's always done that way.'*

As Rear Admiral Grace Hopper correctly stated, 'The most damaging phrase in the language is "It's always been done that way."' And everybody prefers to quietly follow what they have been told simply so that they can avoid putting the effort for improving their life.

In our society, we assume that having lived longer gives us wisdom that a young man should welcome. Unfortunately, nothing could be further from the truth. Why? Because learning how to enjoy life is an attitude and an attitude is always an individual's choice.

Why follow every rule you have been imprisoned in just because it has always been done that way? If the elders really knew how to enjoy life, they would have taught us just that. But since the world is becoming unhappier day by day, it is clear proof that not all our elders really knew themselves, what was the secret to enjoying life. So, we must spare them and learn the path of happiness ourselves.

If you are feeling unhappy, depressed or full of anxiety just trying to meet the 'shoulds' of your society, it's time to break this barrier of convention.

## WHY BREAK THE CONVENTIONAL RULES?

Sadly, our culture teaches that it is disrespectful to disobey, that you shouldn't break (or even question) the rules set by tradition. However, for the sake of your own happiness, it is important for you to determine which rules really work and are necessary to preserve order in our culture and which can be broken or changed *without harm to yourself or others.*

Nobody wishes to destroy society, but many of us would like to give the individual more freedom within it, freedom from *meaningless* 'musts' and silly 'shoulds.' What the limitless person is striving for is a choice to be free from the servant mentality of constant adherence to the 'shoulds.'

Virtually all 'shoulds' (barriers) and traditions are imposed by external sources. We first get them from the society, e.g. you can't do that, that's immoral, that's crazy, no one in our family does that, and so on. We have been burdened with rules (limits) against practically everything…which days you must not drink, how you should enjoy your sex, what you should say when, etc. And our rule makers are often people who *insist* that they know what is good for us.

It is not surprising that we find ourselves placing too much emphasis on what others think. We have been conditioned to do so throughout our life. Before we know it, we become approval-seekers and if our performance in any area is not applauded or recognized by others, we feel depressed.

To add fuel to fire, everyday we are bombarded with hundreds of cultural messages that encourage us to seek approval. Every advertiser of toothpastes, creams, sprays, soaps, etc. recognizes that people are infected with the need for acceptance and so they capitalize on this need to ensure you fulfill your need of approval by purchasing the item they are strongly advertising.

## APPROVAL SEEKING MAKES YOU LIMITED

No doubt everybody likes to be endorsed and applauded for their deeds, but if you 'need' and 'must have' the approval of others, then you become a victim because if you don't get it, you are bound to collapse.

When approval seeking is a need, then you can never confidently state what it is you think and feel at any present moment of your life. *You sacrifice yourself to the opinion of others.* It is, therefore, very important to understand that this 'need' for approval must be eradicated if you are ever to gain personal fulfillment and happiness.

Though you may have grown up following a certain set of rules at every stage of your life, you must not forget that you have the power to accept or reject any rule that acts as a barrier to your individual happiness. You need not treat the traditional rules (limits) as immovable barriers when, in fact, they may be useless and causing unnecessary misery to you. And that can happen only when you stop hanging on to this approval seeking behaviour.

## STOP 'MUST' ERBATING

Albert Ellis coined a lovely word 'musterbating' (to help us free ourselves) which means 'the tendency to incorporate 'musts' in your life.' If you find yourself behaving in ways that you feel you MUST, even though you would prefer to behave in another way, then you are *musterbating.* And you behave in the 'must' ways only so that you get the approval of others.

But remember, when you look for approval from others, you lose the freedom to be yourself. And if you can't be yourself, then how can you feel free in the real sense? Be clear of the fact that *you will always get some disapproval for everything you feel, think, say or do.* Expecting and accepting this fact is the best way out of this tunnel of despair.

Instead of trying to please everybody, start pleasing yourself first and let those who are attracted to *what you are* be attracted to you. As you become willing to release the compulsion to need validation from others, you can begin to give of yourself in a unique way which others will more likely value you for.

You need not be any specific 'something' all your acquaintances would want you to be. Just *plain goodness is attractive* to people.

There really is no proper way for doing anything; there is only what *you* decide is right for you as long as you don't make it difficult for others to get along. No doubt good manners are certainly appropriate (showing how you respect other people) but most etiquette guidelines are fruitless rules that were arbitrarily made at one time.

The only way to create a happy life for yourself is by learning to rid yourself of your freedom-defying belief in limits. From today, invite yourself to live in a radically new spiritual dimension of living a limitless life by *leaving the room of constraints.*

Don't waste time spending your present moments in efforts to win the approval of others or in being concerned with the thought that others might disapprove of what you are doing. Determine your behaviour based upon your own conscience and the laws of your culture that work for you rather than because someone has dictated how you should behave.

The day you start *using yourself as a guide* without needing the approval of an outside force, from that day you will start feeling the most religious experience you can ever have…because as they correctly state – 'Truth shall set you free.'

Stop being a slave of society and experience the wonderful freedom and joy of being a limitless person. From this very moment, *learn to express, not impress.*

## SING YOUR OWN SONG

*Sing your own song of happiness in any way you choose,*
*Oblivious to how it is supposed to be sung.*

—Anonymous

Something soulful

## YOU ARE A NO- LIMITS PERSON IF...

You know you are self-fulfilling;
Finding everything and everyone thrilling.

You have enthusiasm so great
That you make your own fate.

You find no point to blame
And happily play life's game.

You have a purpose so strong;
You never doubt that it's wrong.

With conviction and honesty you speak
That makes the dishonest feel weak.

You look for a person's heart of honey
Instead of checking his worth in money.

You reject comparing yourself with others
Knowing they are all universal brothers.

You can laugh at all things, big or small;
Whenever, wherever, with whomsoever at all.

You never ever need to manipulate
And prefer to clearly communicate.

You have no need to go any faster
Since you are your life's self-master.

You can jump the hurdles of rules
Which victimize you with traditional tools.

You live life with so much fire;
You naturally motivate and inspire.

You are an example of happy living;
Instead of taking you are always giving.

You flow with life, liking it
Rather than fretting and fighting it.

—*Just* Win *Singh*

## Action plan

1) Begin to get your sense of worth from *within* rather than trying to get others to value you from *without*.

> Don't look for appreciation from everybody. Simply remind yourself – '*I enjoy others appreciation of me, but I don't depend on it, for no one else can know me as well as I know myself.* And if they are not appreciating me, it may be because they aren't appreciating themselves either, so they can't see beyond their own pain. I am what I am and it is okay as long as I am not hurting anyone else in the process.'

2) In all fairness, stop having 'oughts' for others, too.

> Just like you, others have a right to their own choice. *Don't expect that others 'ought' to do it your way.* There can be many ways of doing anything and if what others do bothers you, its simply your reaction to it. Instead of saying, 'He shouldn't be doing that,' say, 'I wonder why I even bother myself with what he is doing.' This will always be a more peaceful response.

Willie arrived home with two black eyes. 'Fighting again!' said his mother. 'Didn't I tell you that when you are angry you should count to hundred before you do anything?' 'Yes, I know,' replied Willie, 'but the other boy's mother told him to count only to fifty.'